Destined to Mature

Gerald Derstine

Gerald Derstine
Box 279
Route 2
Bradenton, Florida 33505

DESTINED TO MATURE

Copyright © 1984 by Gerald Derstine
Printed in the United States of America
ISBN: 0-88368-147-1

Edited by Diana L. Matisko

CONTENTS

INTRODUCTION

Most Christians are aware of the fact that there is more to the Christian life than merely maintaining their relationship with God. They feel a sense of urgency to come into a state of fruitfulness in their service to God and for His Kingdom.

Destined To Mature is written to establish a practical, simple understanding of how you can move into a fruitful ministry in the very place you are now. The Holy Spirit is very capable of teaching you and guiding you into all truth. He will enable you, through your personal encounters and experiences, to come into a place of ministry and service.

These messages have been printed in former issues of Harvest Time Magazine and have proven to be a great blessing to countless Christian people throughout the world. My prayer is that your life also may be enriched and your Christian experience strengthened through reading this book.

Chapter 1

BEGINNING THE NEW LIFE

Once you are saved and become a member of God's family, you will desire to display His power to the world. This desire is from God. However, all too often, we think of His power only in terms of supernatural works and great miracles. These signs will surely follow believers, but they are not necessarily of primary importance.

Just as God did not save you solely to send you to heaven, neither did He save you only to exhibit His mighty works. God saved you to bring you into such intimate *harmony* with Himself that you would be an expression of *His will* upon the earth.

This is not how we think it should be, but how He wants it to be. Jesus prayed, "Our Father which art in heaven, Hallowed be thy name. Thy kingdom come. *Thy will be done in earth*, as it is in heaven" (Matthew 6:9,10). For His will to be done in earth, it must be done *in you*.

What Is Your Objective?

What is your purpose, your objective in the

Lord? Businessmen have objectives, farmers have objectives, but all too often individual Christians are uncertain about their objective or unclear as to what it should be.

Some consider their objective to be to reach heaven. Others consider it to be the elimination of sin from their lives and to break such habits as drinking and gambling. Others consider their objective to be faithful to their church or to do some work for God. Such objectives are good, of course, but they are not God's ultimate objectives for our lives.

The individual Christian's objective should be that which the Lord desires for him—*to bring honor and glory to God.* This can only be done by becoming an expression of God's will here on this earth! The Christian's true objective can only be to walk as the Lord would have him walk, expressing *His* holiness, *His* abilities, and *His* life.

God Gives The Ability

We cannot do this in our own natural selves. However, God has made it possible, through Jesus Christ, for *every believer to become an effective minister for His Kingdom.* He puts within us—within *you*—His ability to fulfill His purpose for our lives on this earth, right now. *You do not have to sit and wait.* You can be busy now and rejoice in it! You can magnify God and accomplish something according to His plan, and thus you can bring God's will to pass upon the earth *right now!*

Let's see what God's Word says: "Who also hath

made us *able ministers* of the new testament; not of the letter, but of the spirit: for the letter killeth, but the spirit giveth life" (2 Corinthians 3:6). Notice the positive statement in the past tense: He "hath made us able ministers." Not, "He might," or "He can," but that *"He has."* But, notice that He says, "Not of the letter" (law). He has not made us able ministers of the letter, for this enablement could be acquired by training. He does not want able ministers of the letter, for the letter kills. God wants ministries and ministers of the Spirit, for all things are by His Spirit.

Since the time of Jesus, a new ministry came into order—a ministry of the Spirit which cannot be acquired through worldly training. This new ministry is for every believer. The Spirit Himself instructs each minister, and the Spirit Himself does the ministering.

Spiritual Exercise

Obviously, we could not minister the Spirit without an encounter with God. But there is another phase of ministering that often escapes our understanding. We also need encounters with Satan. This causes our ability in discerning good and evil to grow. We need our senses exercised in order to increase our familiarity with the living Christ who dwells within us, "Christ in you, the hope of glory" (Colossians 1:27).

"For when for the time ye ought to be teachers, ye have need that one teach you again which be the first principles of the oracles of God; and are become such as have need of milk, and not of strong meat. For every one that useth milk is unskillful in the word of righteousness: for he is a babe. But strong meat belongeth to them that are full of age, even those who by reason of use have their senses exercised to discern both good and evil'' (Hebrews 5:12-14).

Spiritual exercise is not provided by training received in schools of the letter. You can know all the Bible, all the history, all the doctrines, all the theology, and not even be born again.

Confidence in and use only of the letter means you're only taking milk, and you are a babe in Christ. It means that you are not skilled in the word of righteousness—that is, God's righteousness and understanding. The only way to become skilled is to take the milk along with strong meat and have your senses exercised by facing trials, difficulties, and tests.

This may mean you will risk error along the way. You're going to come up against false prophets. There will be errors in teaching to contend with. But, as your skill develops in the Spirit, you will avoid being deceived yourself, and you'll begin to mature.

A Glorious Ministry

The Spirit in us will carry us through if we place our complete dependence upon Him. It isn't something that we can do ourselves, but something to allow Him to do in us and through us. It is God's desire to lead us, guide us, and use us for

His honor and glory. We must allow Him to use us.

If we are merely doing nice things for God, we're not fulfilling His plan for our lives. We may be working our hearts out and still be missing His plan. We are meant to be more than a mere statistic on some church roll. God has called us to be able ministers of the new covenant, which is Jesus Christ. This ministry is far more glorious than a ministry only of the letter.

"But if the ministration of death, written and engraven in stones, was glorious, so that the children of Israel could not stedfastly behold the face of Moses for the glory of his countenance; which glory was to be done away: How shall not the ministration of the spirit be rather glorious?" (2 Corinthians 3:7,8).

This glorious ministry of the Spirit is not religion, just as Christianity is not religion. Religion is man's effort to appease God by serving Him. Christianity is a life. It is God's moving through man to bless the earth, to bring life, peace, understanding, and deliverance to the world. Christianity is the Spirit of Christ moving through earthen vessels—you and me. All that we become is a yielded vessel.

It is not saying, "Oh God, what can I do for you now?" or, "Lord, I hope I'm doing the right thing for you." Rather, it is allowing the Spirit of God to accomplish His purpose. The more we decrease, the more He increases—and the greater and more glorious the ministry of His Spirit through us becomes.

We Must Die

In order to bring us into such a walk, He must cause us to die that His life may be manifested. If we defend our lives, He cannot live in us and through us. When Christ's life moves through us, our lives will minister His glory, His will, His grace, His truth, and all that He is here upon the earth.

The world is going to see a demonstration of the glory of God such as it has never seen. It's going to come through the power of the Holy Spirit in the yielded children of God. It will not come by the letter, but by the Spirit. The letter introduces us to Him who is the Spirit of God. This new covenant is Jesus Christ.

Chapter 2

SPIRITUAL INFANCY TO CHRISTIAN ADULTHOOD

The truth of God's Word will never change. However, temporal things of this world must be changed before the complete plan of God is realized. According to the Scriptures, all people live under the sufferings of the fall of Adam. Satanic influence has prevailed and is jeopardizing the very existence of human life.

The promise of eternal life through faith in our Lord Jesus Christ has been the emphasis of the Church through the years. Thank God for gospel evangelists who trumpet the blessed news of eternal hope through personal faith in the Lord Jesus Christ. Unfortunately, many Christians have settled into believing that the new birth experience is all that God intends for them in this life.

More Than Heaven

Those who have searched the Scriptures have discovered the many other blessings that God gives His children. They have found that their Savior Jesus Christ also heals their diseases and delivers them from fears and frustrations. They have even learned that the Lord has sufficient power to convert them from their former human weaknesses, faults, and temperamental characteristics.

Our emphasis in relation to this great salvation is determined by the degree of our need and by our knowledge and understanding. Our emphasis should be expected to change at various times during our Christian growth.

For example, when a baby is born, it has very limited knowledge. Yet it can never be more alive, even if it lives 100 years. We know that the baby is destined to mature into the likeness of its parent.

Growing In Him

By the same token, a newborn child of God has launched upon a new life. He is destined to mature into the likeness of the One responsible for his new birth in Christ. We should rejoice when we notice a Christian seeking further truth, experience, and knowledge. A normal, growing Christian will change his emphasis as he develops and grows into the likeness of Jesus Christ. If you know that you are a babe in Christ, you should also realize that you will not remain a babe in Christ. Rather, you will progressively change into maturity, "grow up into him in all things, which is the head, even Christ" (Ephesians 4:15).

The time has come for the Christian to realize who he is, and why he is who he is, from his *heavenly Father's viewpoint*. During much of our

14

Christian life, we are interested in who we are from our own viewpoint. We are glad to be saved from sin, to escape hell, and enter into heaven when we die. So our greatest emphasis is to maintain our personal faith in Jesus Christ as Savior. It is as if the most important thing in this life is to obtain God's approval in order to have a happy eternity. Of course, all this time, the baby Christian is thinking in terms of himself only and how to gain all of the benefits God has to offer.

Doing God's Will

As the Christian matures, he realizes that God also has a plan for this earth and that He uses people to fulfill His plan. Jesus prayed to His Father, "Our Father which art in heaven, Hallowed be thy name. Thy kingdom come. *Thy will be done in earth, as it is in heaven"* (Matthew 6:9,10). Do you suppose the Father would be pleased to answer this prayer? Of course He would! Then why are so many Christians more interested in leaving this earth and going to heaven? Many are crying and calling for Jesus to come back and take them away from troubles and sorrow. Others are saying that God's people will be lifted off the earth before much tribulation can come.

God calls His people to do much more than wait for an escape from life's difficulties. God gave us a Savior so that we may receive His own life and Spirit. We can stand in the power of His might by His Spirit.

15

This is what God is doing today in this wonderful outpouring of His Spirit. God's spiritual power is in the world today, as it has been since the day of Pentecost. It will occupy a place in your life and enable you to overcome all your human weaknesses. The Bible says, "But ye shall receive power, after that the Holy Ghost is come upon you" (Acts 1:8). This is God's power. His Spirit power is great enough to overthrow the Satanic power now existing upon this earth.

A New Emphasis

Today, our emphasis as God's people should be: "Thy kingdom come. Thy will be done in earth as it is in heaven." We are interested in seeing the Father's will accomplished and now believe it is possible. We know that our bodies are filled with the Holy Spirit and that Christ abides within us *now*. Surely, Christ shall finish the work in bringing to pass the Kingdom of God.

Let us look up and praise God for this Light which has come. "Arise, shine; for thy light is come, and the glory of the Lord is risen upon thee. For behold, the darkness shall cover the earth, and gross darkness the people: but the Lord shall arise upon thee, and *his glory shall be seen upon thee*" (Isaiah 60:1-2).

What is your emphasis today? Are you looking for a way out? Or are you looking for a way to be used of God to bring His glory and knowledge to this earth? As we mature, God provides us with more opportunities for His service. We need to be

16

of the earth. . . .Then Peter said to them, Repent, and be baptized every one of you in the name of Jesus Christ for the remission of sins, and ye shall receive the gift of the Holy Ghost" (Acts 1:8; Acts 2:38).

As a child begins to mature, he learns to use his emotions to become noticed. In a similar way, the Lord brings the child of God through this phase of the soulish realm by the power of the Holy Spirit. Christians living in this soulish realm are generally advocates of the Holiness and Pentecostal movements. These people are many times considered fanatical and extreme, especially by the fundamentalist babes in Christ. Since the babes have not received this experience themselves, they are prone to ridicule it or deem it unnecessary.

This state of the Christian believer is like that of an adolescent. At this stage, the person begins to have adult inclinations but still uses childish judgment and wisdom. This is why the extremes generally occur in the soulish realm. The Holy Spirit filled Christian can do the work of Christ such as healing the sick, casting out devils, and speaking in tongues. He is reaching out, desiring to do the works of his heavenly Father. Yet, he may commit many errors in judgment.

The food for this phase in Christian experience generally comes out of the book of Acts and 1 Corinthians 12 and 14. The gifts of the Spirit become revealed in this phase. Satan often tries to cause pride to control the Christian's newfound knowledge, causing the believer to be dogmatic concerning his newfound interpretations of the Scriptures. This leads to arguments in comparing doctrines and traditions, causing division in the body of Christ. It is quite possible to experience the gifts of the Spirit and yet not minister them in proper, God-given wisdom. We are exhorted in 1 Corinthians 14:40 to "Let all things be done decently and in order."

Some only care to experience the supernatural just to indulge in the good feelings it produces. God intends for us to experience good feelings of joy, but not to make this an end in itself. We represent God to the world and are to fulfill the great plan of salvation for mankind. *The greatest blessing is not seeking for a blessing, but in being one.*

Adulthood—Fulfilling God's Purpose

God calls His people to grow beyond the stage of adolescent emotionalism and into spiritual adulthood. It is only in adulthood that we can actually be a complete blessing to one another. Adulthood is a fulfillment of all the teenage struggles and lessons that are necessary for growth.

We are living in a generation when the mature sons of God will appear. "For the earnest expectation of the creature waiteth for the manifestation of the sons of God" (Romans 8:19). These people will take on the nature and character of God. Hebrews 5:14 explains quite clearly how His people have attained maturity in Christ. "But strong meat belongeth to them that are of full age, even those who *by reason of use have their senses exercised to discern both good and evil."*

The man who receives all his knowledge through books may never know what maturity in Christ means. This is because maturity can come only through the use of exercising his senses to *discern* (not intellectually understand) both good and evil. This is only possible by the power of the Holy Spirit in our lives. You cannot teach people into the Spirit, they must grow into the Spirit and into maturity. This is a process which is fed by trials and temptations and by seeking Him. "Beloved, think it not strange concerning the fiery trial which is to try you, as though some strange thing happened unto you: But rejoice, inasmuch as ye are partakers of Christ's sufferings; that when his glory shall be revealed, ye may be glad also with exceeding joy" (1 Peter 4:12-13). The Christian who arms himself with the mind of Christ and walks in the power of God finds that the fruit of the Spirit becomes evident in his life. "But the fruit of the Spirit is love, joy, peace, longsuffering, gentleness, goodness, faith, meekness, temperance: against such there is no law" (Galatians 5:22-23).

It is in the realm of the Spirit where man has ceased from all his own labors and struggles. He no longer *tries* to work for God, but rather, he lets God use him. He is not only led by the Spirit. He walks in the Spirit. "If we live in the Spirit, let us also walk in the Spirit. . . .For as many as are led by the Spirit of God, they are the sons of God"

(Galatians 5:25; Romans 8:14). His major concern is not trying to be obedient to God's laws and commandments, but rather to fulfill them as an expression of God. This person is not wrangling over doctrines and traditions. Instead, he is imparting the very breath and life of God to the world.

Baby and adolescent Christians will not be able to comprehend all of this. When their time is come however, they will grow into a greater knowledge of the truth. It is no longer a matter of convincing people to join a church. It is a matter of bringing people into fellowship with God. It is causing people to enter into the Kingdom of God by faith in the finished work on Calvary's cross.

Our emphasis must be on the Kingdom of God rather than temporal things. It is here that the world will see Christ in and through you. This is God's perfect will for you. Once the church comes into this understanding, we can look for the visible return of Jesus Christ. He has promised to come back for a spotless and blameless body. "That he might present it to himself a glorious church, not having spot, or wrinkle, or any such thing; but that it should be holy and without blemish. . . .Beloved, now are we the sons of God, and it doth not yet appear what we shall be: but we know that, when he shall appear, we shall be like him; for we shall see him as he is" (Ephesians 5:27; 1 John 3:2).

The believer in this realm will manifest great love and forbearance to all opposers and scoffers.

This Christian will love all other Christians regardless of Church affiliation and doctrine. True nonresistance will be manifest like the world has never seen since Christ walked upon the earth. This is the day of a true revelation of Christ to the world. Let us open our hearts and cry, "Abba, Father!" Let us be willing to grow up into Him, thus fulfilling all the fullness of Christ to our generation.

Look at your life today. Are you living in the body, in the soul, or in the spirit? Even as Jesus is the Son of God, given to redeem mankind, we now become sons of God through faith in Christ. "The Spirit itself beareth witness with our spirit, that we are the children of God: And if children, then heirs; heirs of God, and joint-heirs with Christ; if so be that we suffer with him, that we may be also glorified together" (Romans 8:16-17). Also read Colossians 1:13 and John 1:12-13.

Chapter 3

CHOSEN TO SERVE

"I love God for all that He is able and willing to do for *me*. Praise the Lord! I've been sickly. I have needed much deliverance. I've been fearful. Every time God helped *me*. I love Him because He healed *me* and delivered *me* and forgave *me* all my sins and gave *me* peace."

This is generally our first concept in our Christian experience. We serve God and we love God because of all that He does for *Me*. We are grateful for all that God is able and willing to do—and we are eager to receive all that He has for us.

However, as we proceed further in our Christian walk, we cannot escape the fact that God intends for us to go beyond our first attitude. He wants to lead us on to a concept which I shall refer to as a *double portion*. Hallelujah!

Understanding The Double Portion

Many of us are interested in a double portion ministry. We have been enjoying our first portion, but now we want more. Perhaps you have been present at some evangelistic meeting where the evangelist announced, "Friday night is going to be double portion night. We're going to have you come forward. And we're going to lay hands on you. And we're going to ask God to give you a double portion of His anointing!"

What happened? Well, unless the double portion ministry was properly understood, various ones fell down to the floor twice as fast as they did before. Or, some jumped twice as high. Others felt the power twice as strong—or, at least, they hoped it was twice as strong. Nobody wanted to admit they hadn't received a double portion, so everyone praised the Lord twice as loud!

You may have been there and wondered about it. Perhaps you sensed that these things didn't really have much to do with the double portion ministry. Nevertheless, you knew there was a double portion for God's children.

Yes, there is a double portion—but it's not in falling down twice as fast or jumping twice as high or yelling twice as loud. If you are hungry for it, if you sift out the counterfeit, and if you look to Jesus for His Light, you suddenly *see* what it is all about.

First, the Lord may reveal to you what your first portion was all about—why He forgave all your sins, why He healed you, why He delivered you, why He kept you from harm and danger, and why He has blessed you so! He makes you see that your first portion was for a purpose, according to a plan which He intends to fulfill upon this earth.

"Oh, I see!" you exclaim. "I thought, Lord, You just saved me so I could go to heaven. I thought, Lord, You were mostly interested so that I wouldn't go to hell when I die!"

No, No, No!

He was interested in that, true, but that was *minor.* He doesn't want anyone to perish. But He has a higher purpose in saving us. There is a plan which God already has in the making, and He's going to use people to fulfill that plan. He is redeeming people and dealing with the people who make up what is called the Church. He's bringing them into fellowship with Himself and preparing them to fulfill His purpose.

A Blessing To Others

Properly understood, your double portion from the Lord is greater than the first portion because it enables you to bring life and blessing to others. The first portion was for *me;* the second—or double—portion is for *others.* The greater blessing comes from being a blessing, rather than seeking one. As the Scripture says, "It is more blessed to give than to receive" (Acts 20:35).

Have You Been Chosen?

Jesus said in Matthew 22:14, "For many are called, but *few* are chosen." Where do you stand right now? Are you a called vessel of the Lord, or are you a chosen vessel? Are you completely satisfied and enjoying your first portion? Or are you seeking some way to bring blessing to others? We are all called to the first portion. But have we been included among the *few* who have been chosen for the double portion?

Gideon's Three Hundred

In the book of Judges, chapters 6-8, we read about the experiences of a man named Gideon. Gideon lived in times similar to our own. His people were encompassed about by enemies of God. It appeared that everything they had was about to be taken away. God chose Gideon and said, "Prepare my people. I'm going to bring you deliverance."

Like Gideon, we see the evil plans of our enemies being carried out with frightening success. But do not forget that God has a plan, too. He had a plan in Gideon's day, and He has a plan for our day. However, before deliverance can take place, God is going to prepare a people.

Let's look at what happened in Gideon's day. First, God called Gideon to be used of the Lord. Then Gideon made a call to all the people. Although *all* the people were called, only 32,000 responded. At that time, the 32,000 were *chosen* of the Lord. Everyone had been called, but 32,000 were chosen. They responded to Gideon's call and said, in effect, "We're behind you, brother. We believe that God is able to save us. We believe that God has chosen you to bring us deliverance, and we're going to stand behind you, brother!"

Many Christians today are like the 32,000 who responded to Gideon's first call. They give their hearts to the Lord and exclaim, "Yes, Lord, we want to be Christians. We believe that You are the Son of God."

Response To More Testing

But when the next message comes, a bit stronger this time, requiring a little more concentration and dedication, not so many respond. The Bible lets us know that only 10,000 of the 32,000 responded to Gideon's second call. Of the original number, 22,000 disqualified themselves and had to be sent home. The 22,000 ceased to be chosen vessels and became once again merely called vessels. Only 10,000 remained who were both called and chosen. These wanted God's double portion enough to hold fast to their original calling.

Gideon had to give still another testing that was even more unusual. It seemed that each time another message came, it was even stranger than the one before. It just didn't seem normal to reduce an army of 32,000 men to 10,000 when the forces of the enemy were so great. Many must have complained, "Gideon, are you sure you're led of God? This doesn't make sense!" As a result, 22,000 wavered.

Then came the final test for the remaining 10,000 who were still chosen. This test was too much for 9,700 of them! So 9,700 more ceased to be chosen of the Lord to bring deliverance, and they became merely called of the Lord. This left only 300 both called and chosen. God would give His double portion to only 300. Everyone had been called to receive it, and 32,000 initially responded. In the final analysis, however, only 300 qualified.

God's Plan Of Battle

How pleased the 300 must have felt to know that they were standing with Gideon and the Lord! How proud they must have been! How great their faith! But then came Gideon's staggering announcement to them from the Lord: "Brethren, God is going to give us the victory. God has chosen us, but we don't need any swords or weapons. All that you need is a trumpet and a vase with a little candle inside it."

Now, wouldn't you say that this was absolutely out of this world? God had reduced Israel's defense to 300 men, and now He was disarming even these! Why? So that He—God—would receive all the glory, and man none of it.

Deliverance is from the Lord, not from man. If He had used the 300, how could they have helped boasting a bit? How could they have restrained themselves from taking at least a little bit of the credit? So God took away from them any chance they had of getting credit for themselves. God gave them an opportunity to disarm themselves completely, to the point of simple trust in Him.

You are living in a time and circumstance identical to that of Gideon. If you're going to qualify to be a chosen vessel for God to use to deliver humanity, He's going to disarm you so that only He will receive all the glory. There's not going to be one iota of man's intellect that will get any praise out of this. Prepare yourself for it!

God is not going to let you trust in any natural thing which you think is really making you a great person to be used of God. God gives His double portion to those who will allow Him to disarm them completely so that their one-hundred percent dependency will be in the Lord.

Many are being tested and tried for this purpose. Many face fiery trials so that God may finally give to them their double portion.

What Happened To The Called?

What about the many who were called but not chosen? Are they going to lose all that God intended for them to have? No, not at all. But they are not going to be used of the Lord for the double portion ministry.

The Lord called all in Gideon's time, but used only 300. What the 300 did was for the benefit of all. The 300 were used of the Lord in such a way that none of them could take any of the glory away from the Lord. And through them, the Lord delivered all of Israel.

I believe that the 300 who qualified in Gideon's time did not think that they were better than those who went home. If God uses you, you won't think less of other people either. The fear of God will be upon you.

We can learn from the experience of Gideon's men that the difference between the called and the chosen is that *the called do not qualify to be used of the Lord.* If you are among those who qualify for the double portion, those who don't qualify will benefit as you minister to them.

Chosen Or Called—You Decide

Each of us must determine whether we are going to be chosen vessels or just called vessels. We must mature from glory to glory in order to fulfill a Christlike ministry.

God wants you to qualify. God has made it possible for every believer to become a minister of His Spirit in a double portion way.

There is going to be a demonstration of this ministry such as the earth has never seen before. It will happen when you become a vessel in the hands of God and bring life unto others through every step you take, every word you speak, and every place you go. The same Scripture which says, "In the last days perilous times shall come," (2 Timothy 3:1) also says, "In the last days I will pour out of my Spirit upon all flesh" (Acts 2:17).

The glory of the Lord is coming. May you and I remain among the chosen and give of our lives that others might live.

Chapter 4

FINDING YOUR PLACE

How wonderful it is to find God's perfect will
for our lives! In this discovery there is joy! Your
lives can be fruitful when they are full of His *life*.
But remember this: before we can have the joy of
the Lord, we're bound to have battles.

Necessary Battles

Only in battles are there victories, and joy
always comes through victory. Oh, alleluiah, we
are a people treading new territory day after day—
and it's the devil's territory. When you set foot
onto a new territory, to claim it for the Lord,
you're encountering new experiences. There are
battles all along the way, but we need the battles
to bring us victories and to provide us our joy in
the Lord. In these battles, God is fulfilling His
special purpose for each and every one of our
individual lives. His Kingdom is going to come
through His Church, and His will is going to be
done on earth through His people.

In order to accomplish this, He has invested His

power and ability in us. He has put His *life* within us—"Christ in you, the hope of glory" (Colossians 1:27). Jesus will not come again until His Church, His people, have applied the ability and power of Christ in their lives and have overcome all obstacles.

We have been a murmuring and unbelieving people. We have been crying all the time, wanting God to take us out of this terrible, evil world. But He knew the world would be evil. That's why He filled you with the Holy Spirit. He doesn't want you to cry to get out. He wants you to praise God that you have His ability and power for victory even in this terrible, evil world. Once you become an overcomer, once you become a victorious Christian, you're going to want to remain on this earth as long as possible to do as much as you can for God. Your cry will change to, "Please, Jesus, wait a little longer! Please, Jesus, a little longer!"

A Part Of The Body

Before we walk in the life that God desires for us, we must discover where we fit in. Then we can prepare for our part in His plan. For this we need the Church—not just to occupy a pew once or twice a week. Too many of God's children have been tricked into thinking that God is well-pleased with them if they attend church and say "Amen," occasionally. No, we need the Church to help us to get prepared. We need fellowship with brothers and sisters who are like-minded. We need the Church where there are prophets, apostles,

33

evangelists, pastors, and teachers because God has given us these ministries for our perfection. (See Ephesians 4:11-12.)

We need to go to church in order to learn, and we need to learn in order to become what we've never been before. It is God who changes us and helps us mature. He has placed His Holy Spirit in us that He may fulfill through us the objective of His will in the earth, even as in heaven. What a joy it is to know that He is working this out in us. "For we are his workmanship, created in Christ Jesus unto good works, which God hath before ordained that we should walk in them" (Ephesians 2:10).

Count It All Joy

Not only do we need the Church and the love and harmony of His teaching, but we also need the trials which come from those who don't agree with us or like us. We need to be tested because the only way we can overcome our weaknesses is to learn what they are. Then we can draw upon God's ability and power to correct them. When we realize that we are weak in certain areas of our lives, then we know that's where God wants us to be strong!

No wonder James said, "My brethren, count it all joy when ye fall into divers temptations" (James 1:2). James realized that even the devil's opposition is used by the Lord to contribute to our growth in Him. The devil never tries us where we have already won the victory, but keeps probing our weaknesses to overcome us there. Thank God when your weakness has been shown to you, and rejoice that God has given you His ability and power to overcome.

Step by step, God's perfect will for our lives becomes clearer, and we realize that our goal should be to make His objective our own. Then we accept our battles as His preparation, in order that we may accomplish every detail of His will for our lives.

The power of the devil has already been defeated through Jesus. Now we must overcome all obstacles by virtue of our confession and our faith in Jesus. The sooner we accomplish this, the sooner God's glorious Kingdom will come, and the sooner His perfect will can be done on the earth.

Begin With Little Things

There is no time for us to lose in finding His perfect will for our lives. We must prepare ourselves, learn where we fit into the pattern of the whole, and begin to function as God wants us to function—ably and powerfully. Then we become a vital force in His family, not leaving our function to other members.

Where many of us fail is that we try to be something that we're not. We try to become like someone we admire. When I finally realized that I was the only one like me in all the world, I realized that I had better learn how to function for God. I knew I should fit in somewhere and somehow, and I knew there was an objective for me to fulfill. I could not do anything big for God, but I made up my mind that I was going to do *something*. That was an important decision for me to make.

I decided to look for something little to do. I looked for something I knew I could do, and I began to do these things one at a time. I discovered that it took special energy to try to do the little things for God rather than the big things.

I used to be a chronic stutterer and stammerer until I was converted and Jesus healed me. I knew I could not preach the gospel effectively, but I knew I could pass out tracts. So my wife and I went to Market Street in Philadelphia, and every Saturday we passed out 1,000 tracts.

When I first began to work in my church, a Mennonite mission in eastern Pennsylvania, I knew that I wasn't capable of being a teacher. However, since I was capable of driving an automobile, I made myself available to drive children to Sunday school. I did that for two years. Because of my faithfulness and dedication, the pastor and superintendent made me an assistant to the teacher of one of the classes. Eventually, I became the teacher.

Compared With A Brick

We must be willing to be used by God in smaller areas while we are discovering our place in His plan. An ordinary brick offers a good example of finding where we fit into God's family and God's purposes. A brick isn't made to stand alone. Before it finally is fitted into place along with other bricks, it may have many opportunities for single service. Essentially though, it is designed to be an important part of some whole.

For example, the brick may be placed under a tire when a car is stuck in the mud to give the wheel traction. It may be used by a little boy to crack walnuts. However, the brick really comes into its own when it is fitted into place as part of a great building. Without it, the whole structure would be incomplete and weakened. Here, the single brick finds how and where it fits into the pattern of the whole.

So we, as individuals, may do single things of great value. Or, we may begin to do little things here and there, before we come into a full realization as to just where we fit and how we should function as part of the whole. It is only when we learn how to fit and function as a vital part of the body of Christ that we fulfill God's perfect will for our lives. We need one another to realize God's perfect will. Alone we are incomplete. Alone we are short of the mark.

Do you desire to do things for God or to accomplish a task for God? These desires have their origin in God. The devil never gives us godly desires. Therefore, anytime we see a good desire in our heart, we know it is of God.

Just get quiet before the Lord and look for His desires in your heart. Then you know what to do. I found God's perfect will for my life by looking for the little desires in my heart and for the little things I knew I could do for Him.

By doing the little things that we know we can do for the Lord, by doing the things God gives us a desire to do, we begin to *function*. As we function, we begin to fit into place, and soon we see God's glorious plan for our lives.

We must become so unidentified with this world and so identified with God that His life will flow through us—that His Kingdom may come, and that His will may be done in earth, even as it is done in heaven!

GOD'S GREAT POTTER'S WHEEL

There are failures re-made,
    And drawn from Sin's shade,
At the great Potter-Wheel of our God!
There are broken hearts mended,
    And judgments rescinded,
As they followed the Pathway He trod.
There are paupers made kings,
    In His Eternal things,
When He fashions their lives, in His Plan;
For He molds them, and breaks them—
    And then He re-makes them,
'Til they shine as His own Christ-man!

They are set in His Crucible,
    Where He makes them usable
To work in His Vineyard Divine!
There He casts in a mold,
    Of the God-inspired soul,
Where He opens the eyes that were blind!
He dispelleth Sin's Night,
    And fills with His Light,
Until that soul is illuminated by Love;
At the great Potter-wheel He empties, to fill,
    For the Kingdom of Heaven above!

Have you felt His re-molding?
    His great Love's enfolding?
Have you known the sweet
    Touch of His Hand?
Has your soul shed its shame?
    Have you felt His Holy Flame?
Have you found your
    Life-purpose He planned?
O! The Wheel of our King
    Is a wonderful thing!
It is made for the souls of Earth's sod;
There are broken lives mended,
    With His Love they are blended,
At the great Potter-Wheel of our God!

Selected from the works of Mabel Hogue Baker
and the book, *"Looking Unto Jesus"*—by permission.

Chapter 5

FREEDOM TO CHANGE

"Wherefore he saith, When he ascended up on high, he led captivity captive, and gave gifts unto men"—Ephesians 4:8.

Captivity is defined as a state of being held in bondage or confinement. It means servitude, imprisonment. Captivity implies use of force and a control imposed against one's will. It is significant that captivity also implies that there was once freedom.

In the beginning, all of God's creation was good and free. The existence of captivity goes back to the fall of Adam and Eve, when Satan took hold and brought all these things into bondage to himself. Consequently, there is a yearning in man for something higher and better in life than he finds here on earth. He is continually striving for improvement. This yearning exposes the captivity to which man is subject.

The third chapter of Genesis tells how Satan tempted Eve, causing all humanity to come under a curse. Captivity is a curse. Because of unbelief

41

and disobedience, God allowed mankind, for a season, to become subject to "the prince of the power of the air, the spirit that now worketh in the children of disobedience" as indicated in Ephesians 2:2. But, praise God, our captivity has been turned!

The Prince Is Cast Out

One of the most urgent missions of the ministry is to tell the captives they are *free!* All who are under bondage to Satan may be free. They need only realize it and *believe* it. There is complete deliverance available right now!

Notice that Jesus said in John 12:31, "Now is the judgment of this world: now shall the prince of this world be cast out." According to Ephesians 4:8, Jesus Christ came forth with a mighty victory and led captivity captive. This was done for all who should believe in His name. Praise God, we are *free!* Satan's power over you will be loosed the moment you believe that Jesus led captivity captive. His work was personal, and it was for everyone. Your captivity was ended at Calvary.

In these last days, we are seeing greater demonstrations of the supernatural than the early Church saw. We are seeing the captives set free from every conceivable manifestation of Satanic bondage. The Church is again beginning to realize her true rights obtained through the victory of Jesus Christ on Calvary's cross.

Indeed we rejoice in these mighty works of deliverance. The devils are subject to the anointed commands of believers, the blind see, the lame walk, the deaf hear, and the dead are raised! But more than that, we rejoice that the *name of Jesus* is receiving rightful prominence in this world.

Gifts Given To Men

Jesus turned our captivity. He set us free. But notice that Jesus also gave gifts unto men!

The provision of God is always superabundant. As wonderful as release from captivity is, it is even more wonderful that *gifts were added unto men*. In the original Greek, the word *gifts* means *spirituals*. We have thought of this in too limited a fashion in times past. The gifts given to men were whole spiritual laws, whereby believers could do the works which Jesus did.

By His complete victory over Satan, Jesus Christ caused the spiritual veil blinding man's eyes to be removed. Our eyes were opened to behold the true powers of our God. Because of the mighty victory of Jesus Christ, His followers receive by faith a knowledge of the perfect use of the spiritual laws of God. The results of that great victory have been exhibited through the ages by men and women of faith.

Nine gifts (or spiritual laws of God) are mentioned in 1 Corinthians 12:4-11. These in turn include many different operations and administrations. These gifts, or supernatural laws of the Spirit of God, have always existed. They were clouded for a season by the captivity of Satan, but regained gloriously in the victory of Jesus.

Satan Perverts The Gifts

Until we are delivered through spiritual understanding, we allow Satan to be the only one to use these laws. Hence, we have crystal ball gazers, fortune tellers, palm readers, mind readers, hypnotists, and false prophets.

Many well-meaning Christians have assumed that all supernatural phenomena such as knowing the future, prophetical statements, knowing the minds of men, and miracles belong exclusively to Satan and his kingdom. Without a doubt, Satanic power can and does produce supernatural phenomena. It should be noted however, that this is done *only because Satan usurps authority over God's gifts or spiritual laws*. Satan is a usurper, a counterfeiter, a deceiver, a liar. He can never make genuine use of anything genuine.

In Psalm 68:18, it is prophesied of Jesus: "Thou hast ascended on high, thou hast led captivity captive: thou has received gifts for men; *yea, for the rebellious also, that the Lord God might dwell among them.*"

Notice the provision, "for the rebellious also." It is possible for people of the world, through their captor Satan, to use God's spiritual laws for their personal gain. But the abuse or misuse of God's spiritual laws reveals the need for their proper use to the discerning children of God. God has given His gifts to those delivered from captivity.

Spiritual Power

Spiritual power continuously marked the gracious ministry of Jesus. The gospels are filled with accounts of His mighty deeds. His healings, miracles, grace, and truth, even His knowing the minds of men and their futures, are described for us. Jesus, in taking captivity captive, restored the proper use of the spiritual gifts to men.

Through His death on the cross, Jesus ended forever the terrible strangle hold of Satan upon creation and humanity. Satan holds in bondage only those who do not believe or who have not yet seen that their deliverance has been provided for them by the Lord. In addition to deliverance, Jesus gave gifts unto men, manifested on the day of Pentecost when the Holy Spirit was given for all believers.

God is a Spirit. If we are His children, we will worship Him in spirit and in truth. We will accept His deliverance and His gifts, becoming more like Him in attitude and character. Our walk in the Spirit will be characterized by the fruit of the Spirit and by the signs and wonders which follow those who believe and understand God's spiritual laws.

Just as when Jesus gave His disciples power and authority, then sent them to preach, the one great message continues to be, "The kingdom of God is at hand." (See Luke 9:1-2.) Saints of God, you can rejoice that your eternal refuge has already been prepared and is already with you. God's gifts are free! *Your captivity is over!* You are *free!*

Discerning God's Will

The free gifts of God give us the ability to be changed into His image. It may be difficult at first to understand how we fit in with the plan of God. But as we mature, His will comes into sharper focus.

For example, two men were walking across a huge field. Far off was an old oak tree. "It appears to be a round object, setting on a short pedestal," said the one man to the other as they were getting their first glimpse of the tree which stood a mile away. However, as they came within a half mile, it seemed that the tree had changed in appearance. Its upper portion had rugged and protruding edges which appeared to be fastened to a trunk-like base growing out of the earth.

When the men arrived at the very base of the tree, they looked up into the massive array of limbs and leaves. They had to admit that both of the former observations were a very poor description of what they were beholding now. We couldn't say that those men were wrong in their description when they stood off in the distance describing the tree. However, their position caused them to see it differently.

We See More Clearly Now

The same is true pertaining to the plan of God for His people today. The Church is in a different position relative to the coming of the Lord than it was in the time of the apostles and early Church. To say the plan of God is not unfolding more clearly in our generation is to infer that the Holy Spirit ceased to function in some previous generation. Surely, the ministry of the Holy Spirit is to reveal, unfold, guide, and establish His will and purpose. You can be sure He is doing this very thing.

The Bible reads, "Howbeit when he, the Spirit of truth, is come, he will guide you into all truth: for he shall not speak of himself; but whatsoever he shall hear, that shall he speak: and he will show you things to come" (John 16:13). Jesus, speaking of the Comforter, the Holy Spirit, says, "he shall teach you all things" (John 14:26). Also in 1 Corinthians 13:12 we read, "For now we see through a glass, darkly; but then face to face: now I know in part; but then shall I know even as also I am known."

Again and again you may read in the Bible that God reveals His mysteries and plan to His people. "Which in other ages was not made known unto the sons of men, *as it is now revealed* unto his holy apostles and prophets *by the Spirit;* That the Gentiles should be fellow heirs, and of the same body, and partakers of his promise in Christ by the gospel" (Ephesians 3:5,6). We read in Colossians 1:26,27, "Even the mystery which hath been hid from ages and from generations, but now is made manifest to his saints: To whom God would make known what is the riches of the glory of this mystery among the Gentiles; which is Christ in you, the hope of glory.''

Developing Godly Character

It is expected that a Christian will endeavor to overcome his natural characteristics and mature into the image of Christ. We know that changes must take place within us. A person is known in two general aspects of life: *character,* whether good or bad, and *abilities,* whether few or many. God also can be known in the same two aspects. In *character* He is Holy, and in *ability* He is Creator. With the Holy Spirit dwelling within us, we are changing in character and in ability, growing up into the image of Christ. ''But we all, with open face beholding as in a glass the glory of the Lord, are changed *into the same image* from glory to glory, even as by the Spirit of the Lord'' (2 Corinthians 3:18). Two areas of our life are being changed: character and abilities.

Along with the baptism in the Holy Spirit, God has given us the fruit of the Spirit. This is love, joy, peace, longsuffering, gentleness, goodness, faith, meekness, and temperance. (See Galatians 5:22,23.) God gave us these virtues to replace our natural virtues so that we might have His character.

There is so much power in godly character that the Bible says that no man can look on God and live. Through our fiery trials, we become aware of our need of the fruit of the Spirit. We apply each fruit by faith at the time we need its manifestation by confessing with our lips that Christ is in us, strengthening us in our area of need.

The Gift Of The Holy Spirit

Both the nine virtues of the Spirit (Galatians 5:22,23) and the nine gifts of the Spirit (1 Corinthians 12:7-10) are inherent in the gift of the Holy Spirit. Jesus Christ gives to us the gift of the Holy Spirit, thereby giving us the power to change from glory to glory by the Spirit of the Lord. (See 2 Corinthians 3:18.)

God gives to us the gifts of the Spirit to change our abilities, causing us to become Godlike. "But the manifestation of the Spirit is given to every man to profit withal. For to one is given by the Spirit the word of wisdom; to another the word of knowledge by the same Spirit; To another faith by the same Spirit; To another the gifts of healing by the same Spirit; To another the working of miracles; to another prophecy; to another discerning of spirits; to another divers kinds of tongues; to another the interpretation of tongues" (1 Corinthians 12:7-10). These nine gifts of the Spirit represent God's supernatural, creative abilities intended to operate through His children.

Power To Change

With the baptism in the Holy Spirit, you have received the fruit of the Spirit to replace the carnal characteristics you were born with. In the midst of your testings and trials, God shows your weakness. He is able to reveal to you any virtue of the fruit of the Spirit that you may need.

For example, in your anxiety and impatience, God shows you the need of His patience. You can receive it through faith by audibly confessing this virtue when you feel you have failed in your own patience. In this manner, you may overcome all your weak characteristics and put on the character of Christ. You have received the baptism in the Holy Spirit for the express purpose of receiving power to overcome all your former weaknesses, faults, and hindrances.

God is changing you and causing you to become fruitful. Even if you are timid and shy now, you will not remain so. Though you have been impatient and faithless, you will not remain so, for God is changing you. God has a purpose for your life, and this purpose will be fulfilled. You are maturing and becoming what you have never been before.

"Herein is my Father glorified, that ye bear much fruit" (John 15:8). Through your trials in life, you become aware of your weaknesses, thus giving you the knowledge of what to overcome. Through His Spirit, you now have the power to overcome.

"For whatsoever is born of God overcometh the world: and this is the victory that overcometh the world, even our faith" (1 John 5:4). As a Christian, you are changing and becoming more effective, but God never changes. The apostle Paul said, "I can do all things through Christ which strengtheneth me" (Philippians 4:13).

As you change, His Word becomes more clearly

understood. His character and abilities progressively become evidenced in your life. His plan unfolds for the present generation as you walk in His Spirit.

Chapter 6

DISCERNING GOD'S THOUGHTS

It is vital that you have victory in your thoughts. You must be able to discern the spirits which come to you that you may know how to make godly decisions.

Without an understanding of your thought life and how God has provided victory for you there, your Christian experience may be turned into defeat.

We read in 2 Corinthians 10:3-5: "For though we walk in the flesh, we do not war after the flesh: (for the weapons of our warfare are not carnal, but mighty through God to the pulling down of strongholds;) Casting down imaginations, and every high thing that exalteth itself against the knowledge of God, and bringing into captivity every thought to the obedience of Christ."

Thoughts Are Spirits

Every thought which comes into your mind is a spirit which came from somewhere. It comes to you to accomplish a certain objective. We think of our thoughts generally as being either bad or good. We need to realize that those thoughts are spirits which come to motivate us into action. It is exceedingly important to know how to discern between them and how to deal with them.

Our lives are governed and motivated by our thoughts—and these thoughts come from one of two or three sources. We know there are two great forces in the world today which are opposed to one another and which contest for control of the minds and souls of men. One force is God, the Creator. The other is the destroyer, Satan.

God provides angels to minister to us. "Are they not all ministering spirits, sent forth to minister for them who shall be heirs of salvation?" (Hebrews 1:14). Satan has emissaries too, called demons or demon-spirits. These are sent to bring about our destruction by attacking us through our thought life.

It is important that we know how to tell the difference between the ministering angels (thoughts) from God and the demon-spirits (thoughts) from Satan.

Satan Works Through Thoughts

Recently in a national magazine there was an article about a businessman from New York City. He was well-to-do and owned a very fashionable home. One evening a thought came into his mind that he should kill someone. This thought struck him as so real that he wanted to do what it directed. Until this time, he had been a normal person, but suddenly an abnormal desire overwhelmed him.

He got into his car, selected a victim and followed her automobile. When she drove into the driveway of her home and got out of the car to open her garage door, he grabbed her and choked her. She screamed, and a neighbor called from his window for him to quit choking the woman. He became frightened and ran before the woman was dead.

He escaped, but wasn't satisfied. The thought in his mind still insisted that he kill someone. He went looking for another victim, but without success. Into his mind came other thoughts—that the neighbor who had yelled at him hadn't paid any further attention to the woman. He could return and still kill her. He drove back to her house.

No one had come to her aid. She had somehow managed to crawl, bleeding and moaning, just inside her living room door. All he had to do was stab her with his knife about fifteen times, and she was dead.

A man, with no record of previous offense, had become a killer in response to a thought. The thought to kill was a spirit sent from Satan with a purpose to accomplish. The police caught up with the man, but it was too late. The evil spirit had accomplished its objective.

Thoughts are indeed powerful. They are real. They can motivate us either to enter into an eternal life with God or to enter into an eternal destruction with Satan. Praise God that He is able to show us how to yield only to Him, throwing off those thoughts which would lead us to destruction.

Becoming Sensitive To God

To understand how to discern the spirits (thoughts), we must learn how to *sense* the presence of God and to *sense* the presence of Satan. We need to go beyond the physical matters that we can comprehend in our earthly minds.

Actually, you are probably more sensitive to the activity of spirits than you realize. Did you ever see people fighting each other, red-faced, swinging their fists, when suddenly you *felt* uneasy? You weren't involved in any way, but something made you feel uncomfortable. You were sensing the presence of Satan.

It is also possible to *feel* God's presence. God is opposite to Satan. God is love. God is peace. God is joy. God is as we would describe the virtues of the fruit of the Spirit, and we can *sense* love, peace, and joy. We can feel a heavenly atmosphere, the heavenly blessing, the heavenly joy flowing through our being. We can feel the glory of His peace.

You can walk into various places and discern whether God or Satan dominates there. It isn't enough to shrug the feeling off as being simply a recognition of human nature. A spirit is at work. It is a spirit with an objective, seeking to motivate and control men and women through their minds.

In the same manner, we discern the presence of

the lesser emissaries—the angels of the Lord, or the demon-spirits from Satan. These may be identified because the angels of God will carry with them the characteristics of their Creator. The demon-spirits of Satan will carry with them the same air, or nature, of their originator. When a thought comes to our mind, it is either to build us up or tear us down. If we discern the intent of the thought, then we can know its source.

The Third Source of Thought

There is a third source for our thoughts which is different from either of the two great sources—God or Satan. These thoughts are from our own selves, for our own protection. They keep us from hurting ourselves in various ways. These guide us to eat when we are hungry, to sleep when we are tired, and to look both ways before we cross a street. Our destinies are not involved in this third source of thought. Until we come into spiritual understanding, we assume that all thoughts come from ourselves. Consequently, we do not give them the serious weight that they deserve.

The Results Of Thoughts

By our actions, others observe what thoughts we are obeying most of the time. You can tell what thoughts you have been harboring by observing what you say and what you do.

Are you a complainer, a murmurer, a fault-finder, a gossip? Then you have been listening to complaining spirits, murmuring spirits, fault-find-

ing spirits, gossiping spirits. You have been obedient to spirits who have their origin in the devil. If
you love to praise God, to encourage people, and
bless others, then you've been obedient to spirits
of praise, encouragement, and blessing. You have
been obedient to spirits having their origin in
God.

Thoughts from God are *God's objective for
you!* Likewise, thoughts from Satan are Satan's
objective for you. Satan will send thoughts of
worry, fear, and doubt to cloud the thoughts given
from God. We need to discern carefully and
understand that all thoughts have a source and an
objective.

We must cast down the thoughts and imaginations sent from Satan. The thoughts from God may
then have their full effect in motivating us to fulfill the great purpose which He has for our lives.
We are to *bring every thought into captivity* to
the obedience of Christ. Every thought, every
spirit, is to be taken captive to the Lord. There is
no thought from the devil that is strong enough to
overthrow us. God has made us able to bring it
into captivity to the obedience of Christ through
the Holy Spirit.

Where Is The Thought From?

Before you can bring such spirits into captivity,
however, you must first discern whether it is from
the Lord or from Satan. All of the spirits, or
thoughts, which come from God will carry with
them His characteristics and His nature. They will

build you up and strengthen you. They are constructive.

But the devil is just the opposite. The thoughts or spirits from the devil will trouble you. They make you worry. They are always in a hurry.

America is full of hasty spirits. These are from Satan, insisting that things be done in a rush because time is valuable in dollars and cents. God is not in a hurry, and spirits from the Lord never rush you. Any spirit which drives you is not of God. God doesn't move according to time; He moves according to conditions. He has His plan, and it is unfolding; He is not governed by time in the least. The devil, on the other hand, doesn't have much time left. He's got to hurry!

Praise God, we're able to come out of the clutches of the damning power of time and receive Jesus Christ into our lives. We become one with the eternal God of all glory who existed long before time. Time is in God; not God in time. If you are nervous, over-excited, over-anxious, or hasty, then you know a spirit from Satan is at work. That doesn't mean you are living in sin—but it does let you know there are spirits fighting you, opposing God's will for your life, and trying to prevent God's purpose from being accomplished. Praise God, you can be delivered from these spirits. Rebuke it in the *name of Jesus.* Cast it down.

Because you are called to be a child of God, you may walk in rest, in peace, in eternal life, and in the joys of His glory. Anything interrupting this life in Him is of Satan.

Christ, our minds become sound for the first time. But we must realize that this is true only as we yield our spirits, our hearts, and our lives to God. We recognize that God has given us His Spirit so that we may discern the different spiritual powers and forces which seek to control our lives. We recognize that our role is to chose between them in all things, taking care that we always walk with God. There alone is victory in our thoughts.

Chapter 7

FORTIFY YOUR FAITH

Faith is something coming from nothing, visibility having its origin in invisibility. What does the Bible say? "Through faith we understand that the worlds were framed by the word of God, so that things which are seen were not made of things which do appear" (Hebrews 11:3). What is seen does not owe its existence to that which is visible.

Is faith something important to understand? Very definitely, simply because the Bible tells us that through faith we are able to please God. "But without faith it is *impossible* to please him: for he that cometh to God must believe that he is, and that he is a rewarder of them that diligently seek him" (Hebrews 11:6). Can you imagine pleasing the one who is able to make suns, moons, stars, and galaxies—the Creator? This is exactly what the Bible says we can do. Believing causes faith to come into existence. However, faith is more than merely believing. In James 2:19, the Bible says that the devils also believe and tremble. Now we know that the devils do not have faith in God, but they do believe in God to such a degree that they literally tremble.

Two Principles Of Faith

Two principles, functioning simultaneously, cause faith to come into existence. Faith is neither one of these principles standing alone, but is a combination of the two operating together.

Let us quote Romans 10:9,10 and observe two principles in operation causing an effect to come into existence. "That if thou shalt *confess with thy mouth* the Lord Jesus (principle 1), and shalt *believe in thine heart* that God hath raised him from the dead (principle 2), thou shalt be saved." Notice in the following verse the two principles again. "For with the heart man *believeth* unto righteousness (principle 1); and with the mouth *confession is made* unto salvation (principle 2)."

In Revelation 12:11, the Bible speaks of those who have overcome the world and are in the presence of Christ. Again, notice the two principles. "And they overcame him by the blood of the lamb (principle 1), and by the word of their testimony (principle 2); and they loved not their lives unto the death."

Faith Always Produces

When faith is conceived in the heart of a believer, it always produces results. "Now faith is the substance of things hoped for, the evidence of things not seen" (Hebrews 11:1). Often I have heard people say that they knew of one who had great faith but didn't receive an answer to his prayer. That person may have been believing God to receive what he was asking for. But he did not have faith as yet, or he would have received a definite, satisfying answer. Faith *always* produces.

Through faith, I overcame a speech impediment known as a stammering, stuttering tongue. First, I found a Bible promise that let me know that it was God's will for me to be healed. I believed that Bible promise with all my heart (principle 1). Secondly, I utterly abandoned my whole soul and body upon the promise by confessing the Bible promise with my own lips. I told my friends and associates that, according to God's Word, I was going to be completely delivered from my condition (principle 2). I believed that God's Word was truer than my own physical condition and acted upon this truth.

For a period of six weeks, while I continued to stammer and stutter, I fervently applied these two principles of believing and confessing. Finally, one blessed morning while eating breakfast and conversing with my wife, I became aware that my tongue was loosened. Faith came into existence and caused the desired result. I now am able to speak all words clearly and fluently.

Walking in faith demands constant action upon what we believe. Jesus said in Matthew 21:22, "And all things, whatsoever ye shall ask in prayer, believing, ye shall receive." It was the Word of God that set me free from my stammering tongue. I quoted 1 Peter 2:24 to my friends, "by whose stripes ye were healed." Also Matthew 4:4 brought life to me, "Man shall not live by bread alone, but by every word that proceedeth out of the mouth of God."

Entering The Realm Of God

Faith is not hope, neither is it merely believing. You produce the substance and evidence by acting on what you believe. "But be ye doers of the word, and not hearers only, deceiving your own selves" (James 1:22). Through faith, you enter the realm of God, thus receiving all that you need for your life.

Remember the great sense of joy and peace that flooded your life when you gave your heart to Jesus Christ? However, as time went on, it may seem you have lost that first love. The reason is simply that you quit functioning in the second principle: acting on and confessing the promises of God. "But wilt thou know, O vain man, that faith without works is dead? Even so faith, if it hath not works, is dead, being alone" (James 2:20,17).

Many people sit in church pews as believers but do not act upon what they believe. They become merely professors of salvation and not possessors of the *life*. You must allow the physical faculties of your body to demonstrate to the world what your heart has accepted, thus causing your body to become a channel for God's living Word (life). Speaking of the good man, Jesus said, "for of the abundance of the heart his mouth speaketh" (Luke

6:45). "Present your bodies a living sacrifice, holy, acceptable unto God, which is your reasonable service" (Romans 12:1).

Two Laws: Heavenly And Earthly

The spiritual laws of God and His Kingdom are attainable now through Christ. God's laws of the Spirit are higher than the earthly laws we were born under. All earthly creation came after God. God was, is, and always shall be. "Heaven and earth shall pass away, but my words shall *not* pass away" (Matthew 24:35).

We have a scriptural right to believe exactly what the Bible tells us when it says, "Let God be true, but every man a liar" (Romans 3:4). Also in Psalm 116:11, "All men are liars." This has come about because of the curse. Feelings and ordinary knowledge cannot be trusted. God's Word is truer than we are. This gives me a right to act upon, speak, and believe what God's Word says about me. I can then receive the ultimate that God has planned for my life. God's eternal, heavenly Kingdom laws swallow up the temporal laws which so long have enslaved us.

God has given an eternal scriptural promise that can destroy every disease, weakness, fault, and hindrance in the human race. "For this purpose the Son of God was manifested, that he might destroy the works of the devil (1 John 3:8). Your believing in and acting upon His promises will bring you deliverance and abundant life.

Your need shall be supplied as you apply these

two principles and hold on, knowing that it shall surely come to pass. As a Christian, you are born of God and have received His Spirit. Hence the Bible says, "For whatsoever is born of God *overcometh the world:* and this is the victory that overcometh the world, *even our faith"* (1 John 5:4).

It is very important to familiarize yourself with God's Word. The Bible says, "So then faith cometh by hearing, and hearing by the word of God" (Romans 10:17). *Faith always produces.* "And this is the confidence that we have in him, that, if we ask anything according to his will, he heareth us: And if we know that he hear us, whatsoever we ask, *we know that we have* the petitions that we desired of him" (1 John 5:14,15).

Through faith we are overcoming all hindrances, thus becoming more effective for Christ and maturing into His image. God has given us His Spirit to enable us to overcome through faith. "All things are possible to him that believeth" (Mark 9:23). "I can do all things through Christ which strengtheneth me" (Philippians 4:13).

FAITH

Faith means trusting, when rough is the way;
Faith means smiling, when dark seems the day;
Faith means to know that your Savior will hear;
When you tell of a joy or a trial or fear.

Faith means trying, and leaving the rest;
Faith means trusting, and doing your best;
Faith means living for God each day,
And following when He leads the way.

Faith is a power that all may receive;
Faith is to just God's promise believe.
So, may we all earnestly pray,
"Dear Lord, increase my faith today!"

By Norma B. Jenson

Chapter 8

JUSTIFIED AND SANCTIFIED

Are we able to know that we have entered into justification? Are we able to know that we have entered into sanctification? These are long words, but just what do they mean? How may we distinguish between them clearly so that we may know we haven't missed something that is vital to our Christian development?

For years there has been conflict of opinion here. Some contend, "Once saved, always saved." Others insist, "You must prove your faith by your works." Denominations are divided over this issue. Theologians disagree. Is it possible, then, for us to distinguish clearly between justification and sanctification?

As a beginning, we should understand the *meaning* of these two great words. Many speak of justification and sanctification without really understanding their meaning.

Justification Refers To A Relationship

All of us have many relatives—parents, uncles,

aunts, cousins. We are related to them by natural birth, and this relationship always remains unchanged. In like manner, the term *justification* applies to our relationship in the family of God. When we are born again, we come into a condition which the Bible refers to theologically as *justification*.

Another way to look at it is to say, "It's *just-as-if-I'd* never sinned!" When I was born into the natural world, suddenly I was a Derstine. When I was re-born into the family of God, suddenly I became a child of God—justified through the blood of Jesus. Since then, God has seen me in a different way, as though I had never sinned.

This is a *free* gift. In Romans 3:24, the Word of God says, "Being justified freely by his grace through the redemption that is in Christ Jesus." By this we know that our justification is not only complete, but that it was freely given unconditionally. We did nothing but accept the gift. We could do nothing about our natural birth, either. Suddenly, we were alive. So it is with our spiritual re-birth; suddenly, we are alive; we are justified.

Everyone may be saved if they will only accept salvation. Jesus shed enough blood on Calvary to pay for the sins of every person whoever existed or whoever will exist. In Romans 10:9,10, we are told how we receive it: "That if thou shalt confess with thy mouth the Lord Jesus, and shalt believe in thy heart that God hath raised him from the dead, thou shalt be saved. For with the heart man believeth unto righteousness; and with the mouth

70

accept it by faith. There is nothing for us to do except believe and accept. Jesus has done everything. Thus we become a member of the family of God, *justified by grace.*

Our Character And Conduct

We have found that justification deals strictly with our *relationship* to God—our new birth. Sanctification, on the other hand, deals specifically with our character and conduct, our actions, and our growth after we have been saved. It deals with us after we have become related, after we have been justified, and affects our relationship with our fellowman. Sanctification comes with and after justification.

Something More

I became a Christian when I was twenty years of age. Everyone in my church was very happy to hear that I had been saved and was becoming zealous in the church. However, when they heard that I had gotten sanctified, there were protests. I met some Full Gospel people, and they said I needed the experience of being filled with the Spirit. They said that when I was born again, I had been accepted into the family of God, but my old nature hadn't been dealt with.

This became obvious when one asked, "How do you find yourself praying at the end of a day? Are you praying mostly for forgiveness for yourself, or are you praying mostly for other people and being happy in your own soul and spirit?"

I had to admit that even though I was saved and justified, I was praying more for myself. "Well," I was told, "this shows that you need the experience of being filled with the Spirit—to let God deal with your old nature, your old man. What you need is to ask God to fill you with His Spirit.

This was new to me then. I said, "What you're talking about sounds all right. I'm not doing much good for anyone else, just praying for myself to stay on top. What must I do?"

First, I was told to make restitution for any wrongs I had done to others. This had nothing to do with my being saved or justified, for that was already accomplished. "If you want to enter into an experience with God, whereby you can become more effective, God must deal with the known sins in your life," I was told.

I started praying about this, and the Lord showed me one instance in particular where I had wronged another. Immediately I made restitution. The man, who also had become a Christian, was so overwhelmed with joy for me that he said that I didn't need to make any restitution. The children of God can be so gracious!

Then I began to seek the infilling of the Spirit. When it came upon me and blessed me, it seemed like a roaring inferno of life coursing up and down within me—a glory just beyond words. The Lord spoke to me and said, *"This is perfect love. You have received what you have been looking for."*

I had received my sanctification. I knew it was real. It was beautiful. It was wonderful. It made me love everybody. I knew God had dealt with my old nature, my attitude, and that within me which was always getting me into trouble.

However, when my fellow ministers found this out, they said, "Gerald, you have entered into heresy. You have entered into error. The Bible does not teach that you should look for an experience of sanctification, because the Bible teaches that when you get saved you are sanctified. God sanctifies you when you become a Christian."

I said, "No, that can't be right, for I know when my sanctification happened, and it lasted for three days. It seemed like I was walking off the ground about three feet, and it was so wonderful. My wife can tell you that I was different and that everything changed in my life. I *know* that I got sanctified."

Two Aspects Of Sanctification

The word *sanctification* means "to be set apart, as holy; to give a sacred character to." It is true that when you get saved, God sanctifies you, sets you apart. I found out that my ministers and leaders were right in this—but they were only half right. Not only does God sanctify us, but He expects us to *sanctify ourselves, too*. He expects us to set ourselves apart unto the Lord.

In 1 Thessalonians 5:23, we read, the "very God of peace sanctify you wholly." Here it tells us that God sanctifies us. Then in 1 Thessalonians 4:3 we read, "For this is the will of God, even your sanctification, that ye should abstain from fornication:

That every one of you should know how to possess his vessel in sanctification and honour."

Notice there are two aspects of sanctification—one when God sanctifies us, and another that is called *our sanctification unto the Lord.*

In 2 Timothy 2:20,21 the Scripture reads, "But in a great house there are not only vessels of gold and of silver, but also of wood and of earth; and some to honour and some to dishonour. If a man therefore purge himself from these, he shall be a vessel unto honour, sanctified, and meet for the master's use, and prepared unto every good work." The word *purge* means to get rid of, take away, put it out of your house, or eliminate it from your life.

We know that our bodies are the temple of the Holy Spirit. Our body is a house for the Lord to dwell in. All of our bodies collectively and individually are the temple of the Lord. Now God knows, and you know, that you have some things in your life which you are not too sure are right. They may even be classified as dishonorable—little habits, little sins, perhaps. These are the vessels of dishonor in God's temple. This is what the Scripture refers to when it points out that if *we purge ourselves* of these things, we may become vessels of honor, *sanctified.*

This explains why many Christians are not used of the Lord today. They are harboring dishonorable things in their lives, and it's a pity. They are kept in this condition by their ministers who condone it and console them by saying, "It's all right.

You're saved. You're justified. You're sanctified."

What they're saying is true, but not the whole truth. One cannot be fruitful for God as long as dishonorable things are allowed. We need the infilling of the Holy Spirit to empower us to overcome and purge the dishonorable things, thus making us effective witnesses of Christ to our fellowman.

Spiritual Fire

Do you remember what Gideon did after the angel of the Lord told him he had been chosen to bring deliverance and victory to his people? (See Judges 6:12.) He asked the angel to wait while he killed an animal and prepared an offering for God. Now, I believe God had already chosen and accepted Gideon, even before he presented his offering. Thus we know he fulfilled the first aspect of his sanctification.

The offering was brought to the angel. As the angel touched his rod onto the sacrifice, fire came forth and consumed it, confirming to Gideon that this message was truly from God. This act was the second aspect of his sanctification. He gave of himself to God and realized because of the fire experience that his offering was accepted. This doubled the impact of the call of God, giving him greater boldness and authority to know that God was with him and would lead him. This is what the baptism in the Holy Spirit will do for you.

You will notice that Manoah and his wife, the father and mother of Samson, went through a similar experience. An angel visited them, telling of the special child that was to be born in their household. (See Judges 13:3.) Like Gideon, they were already sanctified by God and set apart for a special service, but they also requested the angel to remain while they went and killed an animal and offered it up to God. Again, the fire fell and consumed this offering, telling them that God was with them and would fulfill what He had said.

It is good for us to see the hand of God move in relation to our call from the Lord. This is actually what happens at the time of our personal pentecost. We lay ourselves upon the altar of God through prayer and thanksgiving and expect Him to touch us with His spiritual fire. He witnesses to us that our offering has been acceptable, and an experience develops which confirms our calling. This experience is the beginning of the second aspect of our sanctification which shall progress and develop.

The Christian who receives this baptism in the Spirit seems to have a greater boldness and authority to speak and witness about the things of God. With this experience, we receive the enablement to overcome our human weaknesses, faults, and hindrances which stem from our old nature. However, if we do not apply this new spiritual life and power to purge ourselves from the dishonorable vessels, our lives shall remain the same.

If we would be instructed properly, we would experience our sanctification and the baptism in the Holy Spirit as one glorious outpouring in our life. Instead, because of varied teachings, many Christians find themselves seeking separate experiences to accomplish varied works of God within them.

Our Part In Our Sanctification

By all means, everyone of us as believers should know that God sanctifies us at the time we are saved. But we should also know that it is then up to us to *sanctify ourselves and set ourselves apart.* You can't be used of God if your mind and life are cluttered with earthly cares. Your fellowman hears your life and actions speak so loudly that he cannot hear what you say. Purge yourself from the dishonorable things and the things which have no real meaning in your life. Lay yourself on the altar and say, "Lord, here I am."

You will soon find that the Lord is using you to bring blessing and deliverance to people. You'll find yourself taken from one place to another, and speaking to people who appreciate what you have to say. They are sensing Christ within you, and He is blessing them and answering some of their problems through you. Only as we become less can Christ become greater within us to affect our fellowman. Praise the Lord!

Jesus, in His prayer in John 17:19, said, "And for their sakes I sanctify myself, that they also might be sanctified through the truth." When we were saved or justified, we were sanctified by God and set apart unto Him. But by means of the baptism in the Holy Spirit, we are now able to sanctify ourselves and become vessels of service in the hands of God. We now become useful and fruitful for the cause of Christ and His Kingdom.

The Holy Spirit cannot lead those into such service who have not purged themselves of dishonorable things in their life. Only those who are both sanctified by the Lord and who sanctify themselves can be led by the Holy Spirit and accomplish the works of Christ.

Chapter 9

THE CHARACTER OF CHRIST—
THE FRUIT OF THE SPIRIT

"Know ye not your own selves, how that Jesus Christ is in you"—2 Corinthians 13:5.

To every Christian, the name Jesus Christ is related to God. He is taught that Jesus Christ is the Son of God. Furthermore, he knows that Jesus is the Savior of men's souls and healer of physical bodies.

A true Christian readily acknowledges that Jesus Christ entered into his life and heart, bringing peace and harmony with God. (See 2 Corinthians 5:18.) As he lives in harmony with God through Jesus Christ, the Christian experiences a multitude of answered prayers, heavenly joys, and godly benefits. Jesus Christ brings many great joys and blessings to believers.

Perhaps the most prevalent truth in the mind of the average Christian is the promise the Gospel message gives him. He is granted an escape from hell and a place in God's blissful heaven. With this thought in mind, the Christian endures his faith,

81

awaiting the brighter day. Thus his present Christian life and witness remains very ineffective. He knows his present human weaknesses and limitations but has hope everything will be different up in heaven.

It is tragic that the majority of the professing Christians have limited themselves to this aspect of the message of Jesus Christ. True, it has a measure of satisfaction contained within but is far from the whole full gospel Christ has brought to mankind.

What Is Jesus Christ?

Most Christians are well-versed in knowing who Jesus is—*Son of God, Savior, Healer, and Baptizer*. We are also well-versed in knowing *where* Jesus is—at the *right hand of the Father and within the believer*.

My question to you is: *Do you know what Jesus Christ is?* All authoritative writers and godly scholars will agree that Jesus Christ is a divine heavenly being. Let us analyze what a being is.

God is not physical but spiritual, thus a spiritual being. Satan is not physical, but spiritual, thus a spiritual being. Man is both physical and spiritual, thus a human being. In each case a being can be identified and recognized through two major qualities. A living being has character and ability. Your character portrays the personality you are known to possess, and your accomplishments or skills portray your ability. Everyone has a certain character and ability.

Jesus Christ, a spiritual being, has character and ability. Satan, a spiritual being, has character and ability. Since man is related to the physical realm, he can recognize the ability and character of Christ or Satan only as it is expressed through a human or physical being. We will not discuss the ability and character of Satan since we have no interest in his affairs. But we do have an eager interest in the affairs of Jesus Christ.

According to correct doctrine, we know that Jesus Christ lives and dwells within us. Therefore it is of our utmost interest to learn *what He is* in character and ability. If Christ is in me, then I know His character is within me, "that the life also of Jesus might be made manifest in our body" (2 Corinthians 4:10).

A Holy Character

One word could adequately describe the character of Jesus Christ: *Holy*. Certainly we all know God is holy in character and that Jesus Christ was equally holy in character. If this is true then we know that the holy character of Jesus Christ dwells within us now, "that the life also of Jesus might be made manifest in our mortal flesh" (2 Corinthians 4:11).

Let us analyze a holy character. The Bible tells us that God's Holy Spirit has fruit. "But the fruit of the Spirit is love, joy, peace, longsuffering, gentleness, goodness, faith, meekness, temperance: against such there is no law" (Galatians 5:22,23). There could be no more perfect words to describe a holy character. The character of Jesus Christ consists of all nine fruit of the Spirit virtues in complete purity and fullness, combined together in one perfect whole.

This tells me *what Jesus Christ is,* in character and dwelling within my life today as a Christian believer. The nine virtues of the fruit of the Spirit are resident within you now, since Jesus Christ lives in you. Christ and the fruit of the Spirit are inseparable. If Christ is there, the fruit of the Spirit is also there. The fruit of the Spirit describes what His holy character is.

Jesus Christ Is Power

There is great value in knowing that the nine virtues of the fruit of the Spirit are in Jesus Christ and that Jesus Christ is in you, "Christ in you, the hope of glory" (Colossians 1:27).

First, we discover these nine virtues are a part of the *power* spoken of by Jesus in Luke 24:49, "Tarry ye in the city of Jerusalem, until ye be endued with power from on high." Again in Acts 1:8, "But ye shall receive power, after that the Holy Ghost is come upon you." There is spiritual power in the character of Christ.

Love is power, joy is power, peace is power, longsuffering (patience) is power, meekness is power, temperance, gentleness, faithfulness, and goodness are power. Each are spiritual and practical realities. Individually, each virtue of divine power can meet a personal need for our life.

We can sense our need of God because of our

keen awareness of our human limitations, character traits, weaknesses, and faults. Therefore the knowledge of *what Christ is* in us can be the liberating factor, causing our lives to mature in Christ. We must learn how to appropriate the divine provision God gave when He gave Jesus Christ.

Now I know there is sufficient divine ability in the person of Jesus Christ dwelling within me. He causes my life to change, overcoming every single human limitation or weakness. As Paul wrote in Galatians 4:19, "My little children, of whom I travail in birth again until Christ be formed in you."

A Spotlight On Our Weakness

Did you know that it takes a test or trial to make you aware of your need of the divine provision in Jesus Christ? Perhaps this is why James said, "My brethren, count it all joy when ye fall into divers temptation; Knowing this, that the trying of your faith worketh patience. But let patience have her perfect work, that ye may be perfect and entire, wanting nothing" (James 1:2-4).

It is during our tests and trials that we sense our need of God's divine provision. In this sense, we can understand that the devil is actually God's tool to reveal to us our human weaknesses and limitations. Then we in turn can appropriate the divine Christ—life provision—the fruit of the Spirit. Remember the devil will try you the most in your weakest area of life. When you know what your weak area is, Christ will become your eternal strength. Praise the Lord.

Overcoming Fear

Through an act of faith on my part, each human weakness can be overcome. "For whatsoever is born of God overcometh the world: and this is the victory that overcometh the world, even our faith" (1 John 5:4). Fears of every description can be overcome in our lives by the power of Jesus Christ within us now.

"Fear hath torment," the Scriptures declare, "but perfect love, casteth out fear" (1 John 4:18). *Love is in God. . .Christ is in God. . .God is in Christ. . .Christ is in you,* a believer. Christ is in His people *now. What is Christ?* In character, He is love, joy, peace, patience, gentleness, goodness, faith, meekness, and temperance.

Nowhere does the Bible tell us that fear is in Christ. Rather the Bible says in 2 Timothy 1:7, "For God hath not given us the spirit of fear; but of power, and of love, and of a sound mind." Your fears expressed in timidity, shyness, and inferiority complexes had their source from the earthly and sensual. Christ has come to liberate all of us.

Therefore, praise God and thank Him for His peace and love at the moment you sense fear and frustration. Speak it out loud, "Thank You, Lord, for Your love." Continue this consistently until the love and peace of Christ control you, overcoming your fears. It is essential you confess this at the time you feel the fears. You will overcome if you can believe. Through faith we overcome. Faith is the victory.

Overcoming Impatience

With the knowledge of *who* is in me and *what He is,* I am able through faith to overcome my impatience. Longsuffering (patience) is a part of the character of Christ, and Christ is in me. Therefore at the moment I commit the impatient act, I have a right to confess with thanksgiving the patient virtue to Christ. True, it was my impatience which manifested itself, but now I'm interested in overcoming this human weakness. I can successfully accomplish this through my knowledge of faith in Jesus Christ.

Confess out loud, "Thank You, Jesus, for Your patience" each time you become aware of your impatience. You *shall overcome.* Through consistent testimony and confession, your mind and heart shall become more alert to the presence of Christ, thus alerting you to the temptation of impatience.

We know the most human and logical thing to do at our moment of weakness is to complain and attempt to justify our weakness.

However, as a Spirit-filled Christian we have no more confidence in the flesh. Rather we confess and appropriate the divine provision in Christ. Patience is one of the divine provisions. Praise God consistently for what Christ is in you, and you shall overcome. "And they overcame him by the blood of the Lamb, and by the word of their testimony; and they loved not their lives unto the death'' (Revelation 12:11).

Through a constant awareness of the indwelling Christ, all of your human weaknesses can be overcome as you appropriate (confess) the eternal virtues of the fruit of the Spirit. "For this purpose the Son of God was manifested, that he might destroy the works of the devil" (1 John 3:8).

A Channel Of Life

The knowledge of *what Christ is* in us not only liberates us individually, but it also gives us divine life (provision) to impart to others we meet from day to day. They have problems. Christ is the answer. Christ is in you to bless them. Christ is eternal; therefore, the source of this life is limitless. There is abundance for all.

"As every man hath received the gift, even so minister the same one to another, as good stewards of the manifold grace of God" (1 Peter 4:10). God has given to each of us a personal ministry. He makes us an able minister of the New Testament. "Who also hath made us able ministers of the new testament; not of the letter, but of the spirit: for the letter killeth, but the spirit giveth life" (2 Corinthians 3:6).

More Than History

Traditionally, the New Testament is spoken of as a part of the Bible. In truth, the Bible is merely the letter of the New Testament. "And for this cause he is the mediator of the new testament, that by means of death, for the redemption of the transgressions that were under the first testament, they which are called might receive the promise of eternal inheritance. For where a testament is, *there must also of necessity be the death of the testator*. For a testament is of force after men are dead: otherwise it is of no strength at all while the testator liveth" (Hebrews 9:15-17).

The New Testament is not a history book, but rather it is the very life and Spirit of God. Only as the words of God become believed and acted upon can they produce *life*. It is this action, this life, which is the *living word, Jesus Christ, the New Testament*. "In the beginning was the Word, and the Word was with God, and the Word was God. The same was in the beginning with God. All things were made by him; and without him was not anything made that was made. In him was life; and the light of men" (John 1:1-4).

The written accounts in our Bible of the apostles acts, or the history and teaching of Jesus Christ, should be considered as the road map to the traveler. Our course and destination of life is guided by the written letter of the Word of God and should be very important to my Christian walk. However, my goal and objective is to daily walk in the vibrant, living presence of Jesus Christ who lives and dwells within me.

Qualified To Minister

The Spirit-filled believer's life will be a literal demonstration of the person of Jesus Christ. We should know what it means to minister the Spirit. "How shall not the ministration of the spirit be rather glorious" (2 Corinthians 3:8).

To have Christ living within us is to have all nine virtues of the fruit of the Spirit resident within us. This describes what Christ is in character. This character lives within you, a believer. You are the only person upon this earth able to truly minister blessing in this world. Listen to the words of the prophet Isaiah, "And if thou draw out thy soul to the hungry, and satisfy the afflicted soul; then shall thy light rise in obscurity, and thy darkness be as the noonday: And the Lord shall guide thee continually, and satisfy thy soul in drought, and make fat thy bones: and thou shalt be like a watered garden, and like a spring of water, whose waters fail not" (Isaiah 58:10,11).

The most keen awareness of the presence of Christ within you comes at the time you are in a circumstance of a trial which demands the assistance of the ministry of the Spirit. This circumstance can be either one of your own or one of another's in which you are involved. In either case, *Christ is the answer.*

Imparting The Fruit Of The Spirit

"He therefore that ministereth to you the spirit, and worketh miracles among you, doeth he it by the works of the law, or by the hearing of faith?" (Galatians 3:5). To minister the spirit (Jesus Christ, the New Testament) is in reality an actual impartation of:

love to the unlovely;

peace to the nervous, fearful, and frustrated;

joy to the sad and despondent;

longsuffering (patience) to the disturbed, anxious, and impatient;

gentleness to the rude;

goodness to the arrogant, crude, undeserving;

faith to the proud and arrogant

temperance to the hasty, unthinking, intemperate.

We can truly walk in the Spirit once a true revelation of the knowledge of Christ is manifested to us.

Peace That Heals

Recently I approached a local business man who was responsible for completing a certain job for me. Immediately upon seeing me, this man apologetically began to explain his delay. He thrust his arms forward and rolled up his sleeves revealing ugly open sores that covered the length of his arms.

Hastily, he explained the nervous condition which had plagued his life with no cure from the doctors or remedies. "The last two days I was bedfast," he said, "my body is full of sores, and I am unable to sleep at night. In fact I have not had a full night's rest for many months. The doctors say it's my nerves."

Something within me responded. He said he was nervous, had sores, doctors were not helping him, his life was full of misery. This response within me was Christ the Holy Spirit, eager to minister life to the suffering man.

"Let me have your hand," I said. Holding his right hand, I knelt down to one knee there in his shop and spoke the words in my prayer: *peace, rest, healing, life* in the name of Jesus Christ. I prayed a very brief but to the point prayer, after which I thanked God for His faithfulness.

Naturally, this man was quite astonished, but he thanked me for this prayer in his behalf. As yet I did not know this man's spiritual standing with God. I only knew he had a definite need at this time.

Two days later, this same man walked into my office with the completed job. The first thing he said to me was, "Rev, look at my arms." Thrusting his arms upward and smiling, he began to tell me how he slept like a baby that night. All his sores had completely vanished on the one arm and the others were nearly gone. "Rev, what can I do for you?" he asked. I admonished him to thank Jesus Christ for healing him. It was not me who healed him, but Christ who dwells within each born-again believer.

This man had an encounter with Christ. I ministered Christ, the New Testament, in his behalf when I spoke *peace* and *rest* in his shop. Christ is the Prince of Peace; He dwells within you and me, making us peacemakers. (See Matthew 5:9.) In the presence of a nervous, keyed-up person, you have the ability through Christ to minister—speak peace, think peace, speak rest, think rest, and thank God.

This does not necessarily mean in an audible voice; but it will probably end in audible praise toward God for the deliverance. The knowledge of the presence of Christ within you qualified you to function as an able minister of the New Testament. "Who also hath made us able ministers of the new testament" (2 Corinthians 3:6).

Joy In Jesus

Likewise in the presence of a despondent or sorrowful person, Christ qualifies you to minister *joy*. Speak words of cheer, life, and blessing, and you will change the person's problem into contentment and joy. Do not agree with their problem by relating a similar experience, hoping to comfort this person. You will only make the situation worse. Rather, *minister Christ* who is joy, and you shall see the glory of God function in the sad person's behalf. This is ministering the New Testament.

Faith Brings Miracles

Some time ago an elderly person was acknowledging his aches and pains, a result of arthritis. He suggested that he did not have many more days to live. This person was believing and confessing his problem and desperately needed faith ministered. Since I knew he was a Christian, I cheerfully remarked how vigorous and strong he outwardly appeared. "Exercise your legs, keep on moving, you are too young to give up now!" I encouraged him.

Although he was in his late seventies, *faith was imparted*. Several years later, this same man, looking healthier than ever, reminded me of the words I had spoken. He said that faith had strengthened him. Each time the aching muscles appeared, my words would come to his attention. I had ministered *faith which is actually Christ*.

Each Spirit-filled Christian has divine abilities through Jesus Christ dwelling within to impart blessing to any needy person. This is the ministry God has called each of us into.

I believe God allows you to be in the presence of a problem so that Christ, functioning through you, may be the answer. The only voice, body, and human element God has to work through is *your body. God has chosen you to be His vessel and channel to bring the solution.*

Chapter 10

THE ABILITY OF CHRIST

"Whew! Was I *lucky!*" Have you ever heard one use that expression? Or perhaps you have heard someone say: "My God!" or "Thank God!" These expressions describe a dramatic, seemingly unexplainable moment in one's life. The best we can say is: "Was I lucky!" or "Thank God!"

What does the word *lucky* actually mean? Is it possible to understand what actually did happen in the circumstance that caused me to escape a tragic incident? I believe we are able to understand every dramatic circumstance. Surely, we believe that God knows all things.

"And all things are of God, who hath reconciled us to himself by Jesus Christ" (2 Corinthians 5:18). All of our actions and dramatic moments are known and seen by God. If God sees these moments, He also understands what brought us through in spite of the adverse circumstance.

Our limited minds quickly respond and say it was really just a lucky occasion. However, a Spirit-filled Christian, who knows that Jesus Christ dwells within him and recognizes what Jesus Christ is, will be able to discern what caused the dramatic change in the circumstance. No longer do we have to say: "I was lucky," or "Thank God!" and allow it to remain a mystery.

Our Treasure

When God guides us into a moment of deliverance and blessing, He functions by the gifts of the Spirit which dwell in Jesus Christ. "But we have this treasure in earthen vessels, that the excellency of the power may be of God, and not of us" (2 Corinthians 4:7). To have Jesus Christ dwelling within certainly awards us a fabulous knowledge of priceless treasure. Jesus Christ is alive, and He is able to function today through yielded vessels who are aware of their purpose as sons of God.

There are nine gifts of the Spirit which individually function to fulfill a specific work in regard to God's plan. These gifts of the Spirit are in Christ. The Bible tells us in Colossians 2:9,10, "For in him dwelleth all the fulness of the Godhead bodily. And ye are complete in him, which is the head of all principality and power." Also we read in John 1:16, "And of his fulness have all we received, and grace for grace." This fullness of God, which is in Christ, is the complete ability of Christ dwelling in you now.

Gifts Of The Spirit

Therefore, we may conclude that the gifts of the Spirit are functioning and are very much alive in every Christian believer whether he recognizes them or not. 1 Corinthians 12:1, 4-7 tells us, "Now concerning spiritual gifts, brethren, I would not have you ignorant. . . .Now there are diversities of gifts, but the same Spirit. And there are differences of administrations, but the same Lord. And there are diversities of operations, but it is the same God which worketh all in all. But the manifestation of the Spirit is given to every man to profit withal."

Obviously, if Christ is alive within His people, His manifestation of ability can be recognized through the spiritual operations listed in the following verses. "For to one is given by the Spirit the word of wisdom; to another the word of knowledge by the same Spirit; to another faith by the same Spirit; to another the gifts of healing by the same Spirit; to another the working of miracles; to another prophecy; to another discerning of spirits; to another divers kinds of tongues; to another the interpretation of tongues. But all these worketh that one and the selfsame Spirit, dividing to every man severally as he will" (1 Corinthians 12:8-11).

Notice that the complete person will function in three areas of life. He will have mind ability, communication ability, and action ability. Now notice these nine spiritual laws of God's Spirit can be categorized in these three aspects, namely: *mind gifts* (revelation), which include the gifts of word of wisdom, word of knowledge, and discernment of spirits; secondly, *communication gifts,*

gifts of tongues, interpretation of tongues, and prophecy; thirdly, *action gifts* (power) which include gifts of healing, gifts of miracles, and the gift of faith. There are a total of nine supernatural manifestations of the creative ability of Jesus Christ which will function through every Christian believer.

Many of our marvelous blessings and circumstances which we may have said were merely luck have actually been a functioning of the gifts of the Spirit. We have received the baptism in the Holy Spirit, and our understanding is now open. Surely we can now recognize that these former lucky situations were nothing less than an actual working of the mercy and grace of God our Father in our behalf. He functions through the gifts of the Spirit which are resident in Christ who dwells within us now.

The Right Words At The Right Time

I once was apprehended by a would-be robber. He pressed a gun into my ribs and defiantly said, "Hand over your wallet right now, or you'll get a shot of hot lead right through you." I could tell by the smell of his breath that intoxicating drink was influencing this man.

Naturally, a moment of fright enveloped me because of the stark realization that I might be killed. After quickly rejecting the possibility of calling for help or in some way escaping this dilemma, I submitted to the demand. While reaching for my wallet in my pocket, I looked into the robber's face and spoke these words: "Do you realize what this means to your soul?"

Apparently God used my voice to speak to this man and prick his guilty complex. He said, "I guess you think I am a terrible sinner, just because I killed sixteen people in my lifetime, get drunk, fool around with other men's wives, and gamble my money." He continued on in describing his personal actions. The more he spoke, the greater interest he seemed to have in justifying his actions. During the course of his monologue, he put the gun into his pocket and used both hands to gesture while speaking to me. Finally, after airing his personal justification in a nervous and arrogant manner, he turned and walked away.

After the man walked out of my sight, a sigh of relief flowed through my being, and at that moment my mind could only say, "Thank God" or "Whew! was I lucky" However, now I know what actually took place.

Gifts Were Manifested

Realizing Christ is within me, I know He did function through me using my voice and body to manifest Himself. Three gifts of the Spirit were manifested in this incident. First, the gift of faith functioned to give me the needed courage to speak the words which the gift of the word of wisdom provided. I know now that the words I spoke to the robber were uttered in the proper way and time. The spirit of my words triggered off his guilt complex, which caused his mind to be diverted from his original goal of getting my money. The end result was a divine miracle. I escaped unharmed, proving the gift of miracles also functioned.

God's people are not lucky, they are guided, led, or, should I say, *blessed*. We must understand what Jesus Christ is and where He is and that He is alive and functioning in His people by His Spirit. Then we will say our fortunate moments were more than the result of mere mystical luck.

What is Jesus Christ? In character, He is the nine virtues of the fruit of the Spirit. In ability, He is the nine gifts of the Spirit. He is all you need. He is divine provision and strength sent from God to change you and make out of you that which God would desire you to be.

"And we know that all things work together for good to them that love God, to them who are the called according to his purpose" (Romans 8:28).

Gifts And Believers

The creation ability of Christ through the gifts of the Spirit will function in your behalf not only in your crisis moments, but also as an act of faith on your part. They will be manifested to accomplish His will through you.

It is in our crisis moments or human extremities when supernatural ability can be expected to function. This is Jesus Christ acting on our behalf, setting us free, or bringing us through the adverse circumstances. Deliverance is accomplished through one or several of the nine gifts of the

Spirit mentioned in 1 Corinthians, chapter 12.

Growing Spiritual Awareness

The Bible tells me that my body is the temple of the Holy Spirit. Therefore, I can expect the Holy Spirit to function through me to fulfill the work of God. I believe He can function at times when I am not aware of His doing so. However, when I am aware of a problem or a dramatic circumstance, I can have Christ be my strength and the answer.

The experiences which I encounter, both good and bad, will teach me the actions and operations of God. I know that adverse circumstances, which in the past I would blame upon the devil, can actually be the means God uses to make me aware of His presence, power, and might. Only after I am on the other side of the experience can I look back and discover what actually happened. I can see where the hand of God has moved many times. Since I have become acquainted with the operation of God's power through the gifts of the Spirit, I *understand. "And all things are of God,* who hath reconciled us to himself by Jesus Christ, and hath given us the ministry of reconciliation" (2 Corinthians 5:18).

My sensitivity to operations of the Spirit becomes more and more keen as I encounter both good and adverse experiences. This is a sign of growing into maturity. The more often the Holy Spirit functions through me, the more I will become more acquainted with Him and sensitive to His operations and movements.

Yielding To The Gifts

We know that Christ is alive and ready to function and help in any adverse circumstance. In fact, in every dramatic crisis that I encounter, I now can look up to Him and expect some supernatural way out. However, the supernatural effect may not necessarily be mystical and dramatic, but can function in a relaxed, peaceful way.

I know that my mind is a part of the body which the Bible declares to be the temple of the Holy Spirit. Therefore, I need not have an emotional outward reaction to let me know that God is functioning through me. On the other hand, I can never be absolutely sure it is God's operation through me until after the circumstance is over. So I must function through faith and trust.

Christ is alive within you. This gives Him the opportunities to function through you or in you. I would like to think that it was my own mind that caused me to do what I did in a particular circumstance, bringing me into favorable conditions. However, I know that my mind is subject to the power of the Holy Spirit. Therefore, I will give the credit to Jesus Christ to whom I have completely submitted and yielded my life. You need not be ashamed or feel you are hypocritical to attribute every blessing and favorable deed to the honor and glory of Jesus Christ. He is in you and is very much alive, influencing what you do and how you act.

Giving The Word

When I am with another person, and there is a need for counsel, advice, or confirmation, I know that the Spirit of Jesus Christ can speak through me because of the gift of prophecy. The gift of prophecy doesn't necessarily mean it must be emotional and dramatic. Perhaps your words may sound like normal conversation. But they will definitely be a part of the gift of prophecy, giving forth the true Word of the Lord.

On the other hand, if I am in a public service where many people are hearing the truth from a servant of God, the gift of prophecy may flow through my lips in a dramatic form. It will alert every mind and cause each mind to take a keen interest in what is being said. Normally, when the gift of prophecy functions in a service, there is good word coming forth from the speaker. As the gift of prophecy flows, it will confirm what is already being said. The sound of a different voice will have an effect upon the listener and bring added blessing, confirmation, and exhortation. Knowing Jesus Christ lives within me assures me that the gift of prophecy is constantly there, awaiting release at its proper moment. "But the manifestation of the spirit is given to every man to profit withal" (1 Corinthians 12:7).

Sweet Communion With God

Perhaps the most common gift of the Spirit that can function at our own choosing is the gift of tongues. 1 Corinthians 14:4 says, "He that speaketh in an unknown tongue edifieth himself." The gift of tongues is a supernatural gift which strengthens the one exercising it.

This gift of the Spirit is needed daily in the normal Christian life. To pray with your understanding alone can only partially meet your needs. However, praying with the Spirit enables you to find a place of complete abandonment to God. His Spirit and your spirit have communion and sweet fellowship.

The normal Christian will desire this gift of the Spirit and exercise the gift daily in order to continue to be strengthened and edified in his Christian life. Also, praising the Lord in the unknown tongue supplements our Christian experience.

This gift is at my disposal since I know Jesus Christ dwells within me. I often feel the need to commune with God. As I yield to the gift of tongues, I speak to Him or praise Him or petition for some particular need which only the Lord knows how to fulfill. Knowing that the gifts of the Spirit are resident in Jesus Christ, who resides in me, certainly gives a satisfying sense of strength, fellowship, and contentment.

The gift of faith is a much needed spiritual endowment which comes into operation at the time I sense a fear or personal weakness. I am immediately aware of the fact that I am a Christian and can go forth in the power of Jesus' name and do what the Spirit prompts me to do. I may feel unable and weak, but I know Christ dwells within me. Realizing this, I will do that which I feel directed to do.

The gift of the word of wisdom may function simultaneously along with the gift of the word of knowledge and the gift of faith. As I continue in this Christian authority and boldness, the works of God shall become manifested through my mortal flesh.

All nine gifts of the Spirit may function through you in a manner in which you will know that you are yielding to Him. "Beloved, now are we the sons of God, and it doth not yet appear what we shall be: but we know that, when he shall appear, we shall be like him; for we shall see him as he is. And every man that hath this hope in him purifieth himself, even as he is pure" (1 John 3:2,3). As sons of God, we have a right to know the power and divine provision which has been given us through the person of Jesus Christ. "For whatsoever is born of God overcometh the world: and this is the victory that overcometh the world, even our faith" (1 John 5:4).

Every moment your mind is attracted heavenward, there is the possibility of one or more of the gifts of the Spirit coming into operation. This can happen either in a sovereign manner or through an act of faith when you yield to Christ to bring to pass the will of God in that particular circumstance. All you will ever need for protection in any crisis or help in fulfilling your ministry is in Jesus Christ who lives within you now. The fruit of the Spirit is at your disposal, along with all nine gifts of the Spirit. "For in him dwelleth all the fulness of the Godhead bodily. And ye are complete in him which is the head of all principality and power" (Colossians 2:9,10).

Chapter 11

VICTORY THROUGH CHRIST

An eminent elderly attorney recently remarked, "I cannot understand why, if God is love, He would allow such wickedness and unjustness to be carried on so prominently these days. Why do we have so much jealousy and greed between world leaders and even church people? Every man seems to be out to get all he can get, regardless of the law and the injury to other people. How much longer can the world continue in a state like this?"

No, God is not sleeping. Actually, all things are according to His schedule and plans. What really matters in this day is to have the assurance that our heavenly Father is in control. It is our responsibility to find our place in the eternal-paternal plan of God in this seemingly chaotic day.

As fears and tensions seem to be mounting in the world, we are able to see another development taking place. Newspapers, magazines, and monthly periodicals are printing glowing accounts of strange, supernatural manifestations of the Holy Spirit of God. Christians from various denominational churches have been seeking God earnestly. As a result, they have been experiencing supernatural visitations such as visions, dreams, and miracles of healing which parallel Bible-day accounts. Scripturally, this is a definite continuation of the fulfillment of the prophecy of the prophet Joel: "And it shall come to pass afterward, that I will pour out my spirit upon all flesh; and your sons and your daughters shall prophesy, your old men shall dream dreams, your young men shall see visions: And also upon the servants and upon the handmaids in those days will I pour out my spirit" (Joel 2:28,29).

Are you awake, alert, and aware of the great warfare raging in the minds of men? One vicious powerful force is battling to retain the upper hand in guiding the minds of men. The spirit of this world, Satan, has had control ever since he caused Adam and Eve to transgress the commandment of God in the Garden of Eden. Ever since that time, Satan has brought many attacks against God's people, and God has accomplished miraculous works of deliverance.

Supernatural Strength For A Shepherd

In 1 Samuel 17, we read about the Philistine armies with their champion giant warrior, Goliath, who caused a very tense situation for the Israelites. From all outward appearances, it seemed God's people were doomed and about to be slaughtered. However, God was already preparing David, a shepherd boy, the least naturally suspected or qualified, to bring about deliverance.

The Bible tells us that David had encountered two minor battles while tending sheep. Supernatural strength came upon David so that he could destroy a ferocious lion which attacked his sheep. The same thing happened on another occasion when a large bear attacked. On both these occasions, David sensed the mighty presence of God. These experiences reminded David that the same Jehovah God who empowered him to kill the lion and the bear would be his strength to destroy the enemy of God's people. David was not afraid, but boldly faced the enemy and brought deliverance to the nation of Israel.

God Is Preparing You

The whole world is about to face a similar situation on a much larger scale. Goliath and the Philistine armies represent the godless forces of atheism and communism which are anti-Christ powers. On the other hand, God is preparing a many-membered David (Christ) as He is baptizing many people in His Holy Spirit. Lutherans, Baptists, Menonites, Methodists, Presbyterians, and others are being filled. They are encountering new trials and experiences in the spiritual realm.

As Christians become acquainted with the wiles and trickery of the devil, they also become familiar with the delivering power of almighty God. These bitter trials and experiences are similar to what David encountered with the lion and the bear. Take confidence now for the Lord shall use you when all others panic and flee in fear because of the crisis approaching the world.

You, as an overcomer today, will be a participator in the overthrow of the godless powers of anti-Christ. The odds numerically may be overwhelmingly against you, but with God on your side, who can be against you? Remember, God is going to do the work, but He will use people to be His instruments. It required only one stone thrown from David's slingshot to destroy the enemy. Surely God prepared a fearless man and then guided that one stone. Do not compare yourselves with others because God has a specially prepared work for you to fulfill. Others cannot understand you, only your Father can.

The world has yet to see the ultimate purpose of the life of Christ upon this earth. Because of the effectiveness of His life, the world is about to behold a true manifestation of the sons of God, a many-membered David, the Body of Christ, the temple of the living God, made up of lively stones with Jesus Christ as chief cornerstone. "Ye also, as lively stones, are built up a spiritual house, an holy priesthood, to offer up spiritual sacrifices, acceptable to God by Jesus Christ" (1 Peter 2:5). You can believe that the purpose of the Church was not in vain. Rather, it is now in the final stages of fulfillment of its ultimate purpose.

Few Qualify For Battle

Another situation where the people of God were able to overcome impossible odds and defeat their enemies is in Judges 7. It is the story of Gideon, that mighty man of valor. The people of God were in danger of being overrun by godless forces. Four distinct calls were given for the army of God. Each time, more men were disqualified until the size of the army was reduced from 32,000 to 300 men.

This is identical to what is taking place in the Church today. Stronger messages, clearer revelations from God's Holy Word are being taught by His prophets. Fewer will qualify for the great battle of ages coming upon the world scene. The messages seem to become more absurd to the natural reasoning of man, and the group of qualified men become less. The Scriptures give us understanding along this line as we read in 1 Corinthians 1:25, "Because the foolishness of God is wiser than men; and the weakness of God is stronger than men."

Gideon had only 300 men remaining when he had to give his final message of instructions as to how to overcome the enemy. However, they went through enough tests already that they would be able to bear what Gideon had to say now. God is preparing a people who will not fall, but will boldly stand and bring deliverance to all the others who turned back.

Wanted—Yielded Vessels

Gideon commanded the men boldly, "Each one take with you a trumpet and a pitcher containing a fire torch inside. At the proper time, I will have you blow loudly on your trumpets and then shout,

'The Sword of the Lord and of Gideon!' Then immediately smash your pitchers, thus revealing the fire torches.'' The Bible tells us that Gideon and his 300 men were given a mighty victory. This shows that God does not need the power and might of man. He only requires a yielded vessel that He can move through.

The breaking of the earthen vessel (pitcher) speaks of the natural man within us which must become broken in order to manifest the light of the world who is Christ. It is Christ the Light who is going to bring a final and complete deliverance to the world. Judgment must begin at the house of God and is now already taking place. This is why Christians are being tested by bitter experiences and trials. We must be willing to be broken in order for life to prevail.

God will allow the hammer and the sickle to break us, causing the true light of Christ to become manifest, confusing and defeating the enemy of God. You need not be afraid if you know your life is hidden with Christ in God. "The Lord is my light and my salvation; whom shall I fear? the Lord is the strength of my life; of whom shall I be afraid?'' (Psalm 27:1).

A Refuge From The Coming Storms

As Noah's ark provided a refuge for his family during the catastrophic age of the Flood, the peace of God through Jesus Christ will deliver you in the mighty holocaust to come. Acquaint yourself with the knowledge and character of God.

Become familiar with the ways of the Lord. Pray earnestly and read your Bible in a new and living way.

Allow the consciousness of God's presence to rest upon you. While the world reels to and fro, your spiritual trials and experiences are establishing your Christian testimony. You are being prepared to be used by God to usher in the world's greatest moment—the coming of the Lord Jesus Christ. The conflict of all ages is at hand. This is why confusion and corruption is running rampant in the world today.

The Lord would say to you, "Fear thou not, my children, for I have called you for even such a time as this. You shall manifest my desire and will unto the children of men. Be not afraid, but rejoice in Him whom hath called you."

"And when these things begin to come to pass, then look up, and lift up your heads; for your redemption draweth nigh" (Luke 21:28).

Chapter 12

MERCY AND JUDGMENT—A PERFECT BALANCE

To the average Christian today, glory is synonymous with heaven. We find ourselves saying, "Well, over in glory land it will be much different," or, "I can hardly wait until I get to glory!" We associate glory with heaven and never realize that glory is attainable here on earth.

However, God's glory is already attainable here in this life. "But we all, with open face beholding as in a glass the glory of the Lord, are changed into the same image from glory to glory, even as by the Spirit of the Lord" (2 Corinthians 3:18). A believer in Christ, beholding the glory of the Lord, can be changed into the *same image* from *glory to glory*.

In this sense, *glory* means God's truth. The presence of God is that heavenly order beyond ourselves. We grow into the knowledge and life of God through our vibrant faith in Christ. The Spirit of Christ is within us now to change us.

Colossians 1:26,27, and 29 reads, "Even the

mystery which hath been hid from ages and from generations, but now is made manifest to his saints: To whom God would make known what is the riches of the glory of this mystery among the Gentiles; which is Christ in you, the hope of glory. . .Whereunto I also labour, striving according to his working, which worketh in me mightily." The apostle Paul makes special mention that Christ was working in and through him mightily, thus giving Paul all the strength, ability, and knowledge necessary to be an effective witness.

Expressions Of God's Glory

However, there are always two sides to every story. In the physical realm, only one side can be seen at a time; nevertheless, we know there is another side. For example, as dark clouds swirl treacherously close to the earth's surface creating turbulant winds, hail and rain, it seems that all the hosts of darkness have descended upon us. However, if you were in an airplane flying high above the same clouds, you could see a beautiful, fleecy array of heavenly splendor.

We read of the Shekinah Glory of God as it was recognized between the two cheribums over the mercy seat of the Tabernacle and Ark of the Covenant in the time of the Old Testament. The term Shekinah means a symbol and manifestation of the *divine Presence*. The word *glory* is a descriptive term of this divine Presence, revealing it in its magnificent grandeur and splendor.

There are also two sides to the divine presence

(glory) of God. There is a reason why adversity, evil, and confusion can exist upon the earth along side of the heavenly bliss of God. Notice in the Bible, 2 Timothy 3:1, "This know also, that in the last days perilous times shall come." Peter quotes the prophet Joel in Acts 2:17, "And it shall come to pass in the last days, saith God, I will pour out of my Spirit upon all flesh: and your sons and your daughters shall prophesy, and your young men shall see visions, and your old men shall dream dreams."

In 1 Peter 4:13,14 we read again about two opposites related to the presence of God. "But rejoice, inasmuch as ye are partakers of Christ's sufferings; that, when his glory shall be revealed, ye may be glad also with exceeding joy. If ye be reproached for the name of Christ, happy are ye; for the spirit of glory and of God resteth upon you: on their part he is evil spoken of, but on your part he is glorified."

Perfect Judgment And Mercy

To say that God, the Creator, is perfect demands the acknowledgement of His mercy and His judgment. A being that is perfect will be equally merciful and just. The Bible declares plainly that God is just. "Tell ye, and bring them near; yea, let them take counsel together: who hath declared this from ancient time? who hath told it from that time? have not I the Lord? and there is no God else beside me; a just God and a Saviour; there is none beside me" (Isaiah 45:21). "Shall even he that hateth right govern? and wilt thou condemn him that is most just?'' (Job 34:17).

The strength of justice is in the act of judgment. Judgment usually takes on the air of violence, wrath, reprimand, or correction. The judgment aspect of God is not pleasant to endure. It can take us down to the very depths of physical death itself. Disobedience, ignorance, and rebellion trigger off the judgment of Almighty God.

Mercy is the opposite of judgment and comes as a result of innocence, obedience, and desire for truth. Mercy is heavenly bliss, loving, kind, and restful, greatly desired and enjoyed. The mercy side of God may be compared to the upper side of the beautiful, fleecy clouds glistening in the rays of the ever-shining sun. However, on the lower side of the same clouds are the dark storm clouds of the judgment and wrath of a holy God. Mercy seems to feed us with divine, eternal life, day after day bringing us into a closer relationship with our Creator God. Jesus Christ made it possible for us to understand and experience the mercy side of God. ''For God so loved the world that he gave his only begotten Son, that whosoever believeth in him should not perish, but have everlasting life'' (John 3:16).

Old Testament Miracles

Israel and Pharaoh's Egyptians. . .
The cloud by day and pillar of fire by night guided the Israelites (God's chosen people) from the bondage of the Egyptians, bringing them into

freedom and deliverance. Notice that this cloud depicts the presence of God. Exodus 14:20 reads, "And it came between the camp of the Egyptians and the camp of Israel; and it was a cloud and darkness to them (Egyptians), but gave light by night to these (Israelites, God's people): so that the one came not near the other all the night."

Ark of the Covenant. . .

We read that God dwelled amidst the cheribums over the mercy seat of the tabernacle in the Ark of the Covenant. (See Exodus 25:17-22.) Wherever the Ark of the Covenant went, blessings accompanied the people of God. However, when rebellion or disobedience became evident, then the same ark caused death and destruction.

Noah's Ark and the Flood. . .

This familiar episode in the life of Noah beautifully shows us the two sides of God's glory. God gave directions for an ark of safety for Noah and his family. At the same time, God's judgment was being prepared. When the ark was completed, the people of the world were destroyed. Noah, because of his obedience, experienced only mercy while the world experienced God's wrath. (See Genesis 6:14 to chapter 9.)

Gideon's 300 Army. . .

Gideon gave the instructions to his 300 men to break their earthen vessels at a given time, revealing the torches within them. The story tells us that the enemy of God's people was aroused from their sleep. As they saw these lights all around them, they became confused and hysterically began destroying themselves. Notice that to God's people the lights meant a clear pathway, while the same lights brought havoc and confusion to the Midianites—the enemy of God's people. (See Judges 7.)

The Light Of The World

Jesus said in John 8:12, "I am the light of the world: he that followeth me shall not walk in darkness, but shall have the light of life." Ephesians 5:8 encourages us, "For ye were sometimes darkness, but now are ye light in the Lord: walk as children of light." This explains why people mock and rebel against the Christian. The Spirit of Christ (Light of the World) is within us, lighting our pathway from glory to glory. At the same time, it is bringing judgment to those who are without this light (Christ).

We know there are two sides to the glory of God—mercy and judgment. To the obedient is heavenly mercy and bliss, while to the disobedient is wrath and judgment. Your unsaved friends sense the presence of God in your life and try to disturb you because they are already disturbed by the Christ in you.

Every new step of spiritual growth that you attain will give off a reaction of spiritual turbulence to someone else. This reaction of the other person will be God's instrument to establish, test, and protect this new truth of glory in your life. We describe this as a trial. This is how persecution comes to the believer.

Judgment Will Come

As the Church (Body of Christ) is being perfected, we will see more and more confusion and turbulence among the nations of the world. The fact that we see the world in a troubled condition is proof that God's people are being made ready to rule and reign.

As the individual Christian is tested and tried, so also the Church as a whole shall go through a great testing and persecution to prove itself capable and worthy to stand every test. "But ye are a chosen generation, a royal priesthood, an holy nation, a peculiar people; that ye should show forth the praises of him who hath called you out of darkness into his marvelous light" (1 Peter 2:9). Christ through the Church is the answer to the world's dilemma.

Saints, you need not be afraid. Rejoice and praise God for your redemption to inherit the earth. "The earth is the Lord's, and the fulness thereof; the world, and they that dwell therein" (Psalm 24:1). We, as the children of light, are not afraid of the destruction which is coming upon the earth for we have already overcome. Hallelujah! We know the mercy side of God's great *Shekinah Glory*.

Chapter 13

BECOMING AN EXPRESSION OF CHRIST

Your life is radiating the expression of one of two great spiritual powers. Your conversation and countenance are indicators revealing whose servant you are. "Know ye not, that to whom ye yield yourselves servants to obey, his servants ye are to whom ye obey: whether of sin unto death, or of obedience unto righteousness?" (Romans 6:16).

Did you know it's within your own personal power to choose a certain path of life? Your walk and talk is daily expressing to others whose servant you are. Did you ever analyze your normal conversation for a full day at the close of the day? Your words to others were either building or destroying. We should know whose expression we are promoting through our lives.

The above Bible quotation reveals the possibility of being servants of sin unto *death* and/or servants of obedience unto *righteousness*. But you would not suspect a Christian to be a servant of sin.

My challenge to you again is to look at yourself.

What does your countenance express, and what does your conversation expose? Do the words you speak carry an air of disdain, murmur, complaint, and dissatisfaction? Or do you discover yourself lifted with thoughts of song, inspiration, and words of life and encouragement to others?

"The words of a wise man's mouth are gracious; but the lips of a fool will swallow up himself" (Ecclesiastes 10:12). "Who is a wise man and endued with knowledge among you? Let him shew out of a good conversation his works with meekness of wisdom" (James 3:13). *The words you speak indicate what master you are serving.*

As a Christian, who am I? According to the Bible, I am not my own—I've been bought. "For ye are bought with a price: therefore glorify God in your body and in your spirit, which are God's" (1 Corinthians 6:20).

This lets me know my life belongs to God. I'm His child, yes actually His son. "And if children, then heirs; heirs of God, and joint heirs with Christ; if so be that we suffer with him, that we may be also glorified together" (Romans 8:17). Because I know the Scripture says I am His child, son and heir, I further know that God is my Father. "For you have not received the spirit of bondage again to fear; but ye have received the Spirit of adoption, whereby, we cry, Abba, Father" (Romans 8:15).

Now I am interested in changing more and becoming that which my Heavenly Father intends for me to be. I want to be the *expression of God* upon this earth since a new awareness is upon my life of being His child. I believe heavenly life can radiate and be expressed through my words and countenance if I am certain my life is God's possession.

Importance Of Obedience

Obedience to the commandments and Holy Word of God illuminates and enlightens our inner being. We receive the knowledge required to walk in harmony with God the Creator. Our attitude and motives become affected. This transforms our inner character causing us to become pure and guileless. Desire to know God's will and commandments. Study the Word of God.

Any Christian that is desiring to overcome himself, change his character, and become Christlike will naturally become branded as a fanatic. The Bible says, "In everything give thanks: for this is the will of God in Christ Jesus concerning you" (1 Thessalonians 5:18). It appears that it would be proper to give thanks regardless of what type circumstance comes into our pathway. If this were so, could it be that giving thanks even in adverse circumstances changes the situation?

Again the Bible says, "By him therefore let us offer the sacrifice of praise to God continually, that is, the fruit of our lips giving thanks to his name" (Hebrews 13:15). This verse seems to imply that it is possible and proper for us to offer praise to God which perhaps takes discipline and determination above our normal feeling. Furthermore, it appears that God has given us the provision through Christ to give us the power since this verse states *by Him*.

Christians have been prone to feel that it is possible to become overly emotional in their worship toward God. I would say we ought to discipline ourselves and literally *channel our emotions* to worship and praise God. All people are emotional. Without emotion you would express no life whatsoever. Certain people display their emotions in the extreme toward one particular emphasis or the other, and of course they are then branded as fanatics.

Any Christian who is desiring to overcome himself, change his character, and become Christlike will naturally become branded as a fanatic in the eyes of the average churchgoing Christian. However, we are discovering that our words do more than reveal to us what we actually are. They also are a means to assist us to overcome what we are and become like what our words say that we are. Jesus said, "Man shall not live by bread alone, but by every word that proceedeth out of the mouth of God" (Matthew 4:4). This verse implies that the Word of God brings life.

Since this is true, and I am God's son and have His Spirit dwelling within, I know that the words I speak can be life-giving. God dwells within me and therefore His Word properly spoken through my lips could exact a change not only in my life, but also in the lives of others to whom I talk.

I believe we ought to praise the Lord audibly and encourage ourselves to speak words of thanksgiving and praise daily. We cannot over emphasize the importance of audibly speaking words of praise. We notice that David in the Book of Psalms on many occasions would say, "O bless the Lord, O my soul and all that is within me, bless his Holy name." David was encouraging himself, his own emotions and spirit, to praise the Lord. According to his writings, we know he literally spoke them. My admonition to you is to join with David and the host of other Spirit-filled Christians. Discipline yourselves to say, "Praise the Lord!" "Thank you, Jesus," "Glory to God," "Hallelujah," and other such related praises to God.

When you speak words of praise you are actually stirring up the very life and spirit of Jesus Christ within you. You then begin to receive the benefits of His presence which gives you heavenly life. It is one thing to know that, according to the Scriptures, Christ lives within you. However, it is another thing to actually speak words of praise with your own lips about the Spirit of Jesus Christ. This expression of Jesus Christ and His blessing in your testimony will bring an overcoming process into your emotions, your character, and your human nature. It will cause your life to become the expression of heaven's life upon this earth.

I know some will say, "But is this necessary and is it that important?" Yes, it is very important because we are living in the end time. Any knowledge that can be gained in bringing us closer to the presence of God will cause us to live with a purpose and objective, bringing blessing to many and fruit to God's Kingdom. Let the lukewarm Christian say you are overly emotional or a fanatic. You will begin to sense in a new way the true expression and life of the Kingdom of God. Your countenance will be influenced and the life you display will be desired by others because the words you speak will carry with them *creation life*.

If you do not discipline your speech in praises toward God, you will discover that the words you speak most frequently will be describing your earthly carnal realm, demanding encouragement from others. The Bible says: "And they overcame him by the blood of the Lamb, and by the word of their testimony; and they loved not their lives unto the death" (Revelation 12:11). Again this is an indication that our speech or testimony is a part of the process to enable us to be overcomers and move into a new dimension of fruitful and blessed living.

Freedom Through Praise

Because of my introverted and reserved nature, I found it necessary to go through spiritual warfare before I could be set free. I went far out into the woods, where I knew no one would hear me and shouted, *"Hallelujah."* This certainly did not come naturally, nor was it easy; but I wanted to overcome my timidity and shyness. I shouted "Hallelujah" at least three times as strongly and loudly as I could to overcome this timid condition. It is hard to explain what happened, but I know something within me opened up and gave me a new release and understanding. Today, I thank God that He gave me the courage and the faith to accomplish this feat.

Biblical Emotions

Let us look at some expressions of emotion in Old Testament times. During the rebuilding of the temple, many Israelites behaved like today's "fanatics."

"And all the people shouted with a great shout, when they praised the Lord, because the foundation of the house of the Lord was laid" (Ezra 3:11).

"And Ezra blessed the Lord, the great God. And all the people answered Amen, Amen, with lifting up their hands: and they bowed their heads, and worshipped the Lord with their faces to the ground" (Nehemiah 8:6).

"Let them shout for joy, and be glad, that favour my righteous cause" (Psalm 35:27).

"The eyes of the Lord are upon the righteous, and his ears are open unto their cry. . . .The righteous cry and the Lord heareth, and delivereth them out of all their troubles" (Psalm 34:15,17).

"Cry out and shout, thou inhabitant of Zion: for great is the Holy One of Israel in the midst of thee" (Isaiah 12:6).

"Evening, and morning, and at noon, will I pray, and cry aloud: and he shall hear my voice" (Psalm 55:17).

"For the joy of the Lord is your strength" (Nehemiah 8:10).

"Rejoice in the Lord, O ye righteous: for Praise is comely for the upright" (Psalm 33:1).

Jesus expressed His emotions openly also. "Then cried Jesus in the temple as He taught" (John 7:28).

"And Jesus cried with a loud voice, and gave up the ghost" (Mark 15:37).

"Rejoice ye in that day, and leap for joy: for, behold, your reward is great in heaven" (Luke 6:23).

"In that hour Jesus rejoiced in spirit" (Luke 10:21).

My admonition to you, Christian, is to discipline yourself to express praises and thanksgiving toward God for *all* things. This not only brings healing to your physical body, but it will bring glory and honor to God and His Kingdom. You will enjoy living.

"Let everything that hath breath praise the Lord. Praise ye the Lord" (Psalm 150:6).

Chapter 14

REACHING OUT TO GIVE

"Please don't ask me because I just don't know how to do that. There are others who are more capable than me. Ask him to do it, not me." How many times have Christians wriggled out of an opportunity for Christian service merely because they thought they couldn't do it. The reason they said they couldn't do it perhaps was because they never saw themselves in that particular situation before.

There is always that certain sense of fear in attempting to do a thing for the first time. Somehow it seems to have become a very common thing for the majority of Christians to feel that they just are not gifted in accomplishing Christian services effectively. However, you cannot afford to continue believing this way because of certain established facts in the Scriptures.

A Change Has Happened

"Therefore if any man be in Christ, he is a new creature: old things are passed away; behold, all

•

things are become new. And all things are of God, who hath reconciled us to himself by Jesus Christ, and hath given to us the ministry of reconciliation" (2 Corinthians 5:17,18).

These verses reveal to us that a change has taken place and that we should no longer continue thinking as we used to think. We should expect definite changes to begin to take place in all areas of our life. Remember, you will experience more than one change because you need many changes in order to bring you into the image of Jesus Christ. "But we all, with open face beholding as in a glass the glory of the Lord, are changed into the same image from glory to glory, even as by the Spirit of the Lord" (2 Corinthians 3:18).

Christ Within The Believer

We are very much aware of our weaknesses and imperfections and realize our inabilities toward godly service. However, a very liberating fact stands out in Colossians 1:27, "To whom God would make known what is the riches of the glory of this mystery among the Gentiles; which is Christ in you, the hope of glory." In verse 29, of the same chapter, the Apostle Paul says this Christ was working in and through him mightily. "Whereunto I also labour, striving according to his workings, which worketh in me mightily."

Again the Scriptures say in Colossians 3:2,3, "Set your affection on things above, not on things on the earth. For ye are dead, and your life is hid with Christ in God." These verses express the thought that Christ is actually living in us and becomes the motivating force within us for a specific purpose.

Keep in mind that the main purpose of your being a Christian is not merely to go to heaven, even though this is an established truth in the end; but the primary factor is that you have *now* become *a new creature* in Christ to perform *a new work* for Christ because of the *new life of Christ* which dwells within us. "Being confident of this very thing, that he which hath begun a good work in you will perform it until the day of Jesus Christ" (Philippians 1:6).

You have been purchased by God for a purpose. "What? know ye not that your body is the temple of the Holy Ghost which is in you, which ye have of God, and ye are not your own? For ye are bought with a price: therefore glorify God in your body, and in your spirit, which are God's" (1 Corinthians 6:19,20).

Did you realize that God is going to use you to bring to pass the fulfillment of the Lord's Prayer "Thy kingdom come. Thy will be done in earth, as it is in heaven" (Matthew 6:10)? I believe what Jesus prayed shall surely come to pass upon this earth. We are going to be the instruments in the hands of God to accomplish this because of the great success of the cross of Christ.

The death of Jesus Christ on Mount Calvary was by no means in vain. He actually was resurrected, and the express purpose of His resurrection was to equip and empower you and me with the *same*

131

life and spirit as was in Himself given to Him by God the Father. This fact gives believers the responsibility of actually believing that He dwells within us for a purpose and the desire to live like it was true.

Nothing Is Impossible

On the day of Pentecost, the Holy Spirit was given by Jesus Christ to all His followers to empower them to be active witnesses of the glories of God. They had also realized that they could do all things through Christ who was strengthening them. Thus, the apostle Paul was able to freely declare in Philippians 4:13, "I can do all things through Christ which strengtheneth me."

There is absolutely nothing impossible for you since Christ has become your strength and life. You cannot comprehend the truest meaning and depths of all this unless you have had an actual encounter with the Holy Spirit. I sincerely advocate there needs to be a definite seeking on the part of every believer in Christ to experience a personal Pentecost.

The glorious knowledge of Christ dwelling in us gives us faith to believe that nothing is impossible to us anymore. All true Christians desire to be workers for Christ and to prove the effectiveness of the Spirit of God within them. It is now within our very nature (divine nature) to express the will of God through our lives.

This all adds up to the realization of the fact that we need never say, "No, I can't do that" anymore.

Although we feel in our natural strength we are unable to do a certain thing for the Lord, we immediately recognize another fact: Christ is dwelling in us by the Holy Ghost to accomplish that which we felt we couldn't do.

This is a very serious truth for you as a Christian. You have no excuse. This is why Jesus Christ gave you the Holy Ghost—to make out of you that which you have never been before.

As a normal Christian, you are going to go through processes of change from year to year because the Holy Ghost is making a new creature out of you in many areas of your life. All this is essential to cause you to become fruitful. God is going to look at your fruit to determine your eternal place in His Kingdom. You must quit excusing yourself from Christian activity merely because of your timidity and fears. You must apply the fact of the work of the Holy Spirit in your life, or you take the name of the Lord in vain.

You must believe that Christ is your life and strength today. Allow yourself to get into situations where you know that Christ must become God for you. Confess what the Word of God says, not what you think. You cannot think in eternal terms, but Christ can. Christ is in you. Read His Word, and learn to confess His Word. Become like Him. Attempt to do things which you never did before, and do them in the name of Jesus. Of course, all is done for the building up of the Kingdom of God.

Time—Your Most Important Asset

What you do with the short remaining time upon this earth will determine the size of your mansion in the Kingdom of God. Time is running out. "Only one life, 'twill soon be past; only what's done for Christ will last." Don't believe yourself, believe Christ. "Nay, in all these things we are more than conquerors through him that loved us" (Romans 8:37).

You are becoming what you have never been before. "For whatsoever is born of God overcometh the world: and this is the victory that overcometh the world, even our faith" (1 John 5:4). "Ye are of God, little children, and have overcome them: because greater is he (Christ) that is in you, than he (Satan, ourselves) that is in the world" (1 John 4:4).

It is all right for you to say you believe you cannot do it when asked. Then go ahead and do it anyway in the name of Jesus. However, it is absolutely wrong to say you cannot do it and then refuse to attempt it. How do you know you cannot do it if you never even attempt it? Let Christ become your strength in all situations, and He will reveal Himself through you. But you must make room for Him to work through you. Be willing to present your bodies a living sacrifice unto God, and He will use you now. "I beseech you therefore, brethren, by the mercies of God, that ye present your bodies a living sacrifice, holy, acceptable unto God, which is your reasonable service"

(Romans 12:1).

You can do all things through Christ—believe God now!

Chapter 15

MINISTERING CHRIST

"Who also hath made us able ministers of the new testament; not of the letter but of the spirit: for the letter killeth, but the spirit giveth life"—2 Corinthians 3:6.

Generally, when one receives the baptism in the Holy Spirit, joy is the first virtue experienced. Why? Simply because joy is the most sensational, the most enjoyable to the flesh. When joy is there, you're most likely to sing or praise God.

But when the joy leaves, there may be a concern that the Holy Spirit Himself has left. Satan will be right at your shoulder to tell you that—but you know better. You know that the ministry of the Spirit is not always joy. Neither is it always peace, or always any one thing outstanding to the exclusion of others. It is also meekness and temperance.

Longsuffering, for example, is the opposite sensation-wise of joy. When someone comes against you, you need an anointing of longsuffering. Joy may become hardly noticeable. That's not when you need to praise the Lord, but to be quiet, to be still, to hold steady. God gives us this anointing of longsuffering to hold us steady, to cause us to remain Christlike in every adverse situation.

Joy is reality. So is longsuffering. Love is reality. So is meekness. So is patience. These cannot be handled, seen, or touched physically—but they are real nevertheless. They are spirit, and they are life. Each of the spiritual qualities of the Lord is in you now, if you have received the Holy Spirit in your life. They are in you because they are in Christ, and Christ is in you. They are your enablement, your ability.

The Fruit Is Evident

No matter what situation you're in, if you will stop and be still, you can see one or more of these nine virtues in operation. As needed there will be upon you the proper anointing of joy, peace, love, meekness, temperance, faith, longsuffering, goodness, and gentleness. The Spirit of God consists of these virtues, and by these we know the Spirit of God is present and is moving.

The spirit of Satan exhibits opposite characteristics—hatred instead of love, sadness instead of joy, fear instead of peace, impatience instead of longsuffering, evil instead of goodness, unbelief instead of faith, self-indulgence instead of temperance, boastfulness instead of meekness, and cruelty instead of gentleness.

God seeks to bring us into complete harmony with Himself, so that there may be a limitless source of supply of His Spirit. Every virtue of His

Spirit is limitless. There is no limit to love, for example. There is to be no limit to your ministry of the Spirit, as Christ who is eternal abides in us.

Ministering His Spirit

We have been given the Spirit of Christ to impart His Spirit to others. We've been given these wonderful nine virtues of God's Holy Spirit to give out to other people. This is what He wants us to do when we minister the Spirit. We are to minister His peace to those in distress; His joy to the brokenhearted; His love where hatred rears its ugly head.

Has someone ever said to you, "Oh, I just feel so bad today; I don't know whether I can stand it or not. I feel like giving up"? Their faith was weak and you knew it. They were discouraged and weary.

You could have made matters much worse by responding, "You know, I don't feel so good myself. Things have really been rough!" Instead of helping, you hindered, if you responded in that way. Instead of ministering God's Spirit, you ministered Satan's spirit. You joined yourself with the problem and made a bigger problem. You should have yielded to *Christ* who is in you, and Christ is the answer.

When someone complains, we know it's time to minister the proper virtue of God's Holy Spirit. For this purpose, we yield our voice, our body, and mind to one or more of His virtues so that the Spirit of Christ may be ministered.

When the Holy Spirit comes into us, we know that the fruit of the Spirit is present. And we know what that fruit is and why it is there. It is not our virtues we are to minister, but His, and His can be ministered simply by faith.

When we ourselves become impatient, we know that our own patience failed. We know that we need God's patience, in place of ours, to overcome. And we know that His patience is there because His Spirit is there, and the fruit of His Spirit includes patience (longsuffering). We have only to thank Him for it, and it's in operation. The Spirit Himself ministers to our need.

When any of these virtues are needed in our contacts with others. They are there because He is there, and they become operative in response to our faith.

Just keep believing. Keep confessing what you believe in your heart, and you will see the salvation of God. He is in you to deliver you by His Spirit from any attack of Satan, and He is in you that others may be ministered to in like fashion.

When Christ came into your life, He changed you, and He's still changing you. There's no end to it. I don't know where it will stop, even in the ages of glory to come.

I have discovered that there is nothing impossible. If I receive a desire to do something for God, I know that desire can be fulfilled. As children of God, our desires come from Him, and if we know our desires come from Him then we know He can fulfill them. The Lord has enabled me to do many things in this way when I yield to His presence, to His Spirit.

Harmony With God

"Therefore if any man be in Christ, he is a new creature: old things are passed away; behold, all things are become anew. And all things are of God, who hath reconciled us to himself by Jesus Christ, and hath given to us the ministry of reconciliation" (2 Corinthians 5:17,18).

Here is wonderful news, for in reconciliation God seeks to bring us into fellowship with Him. Through us He seeks to bring others into like fellowship. God seeks to bring us into harmony with Himself and to give us a ministry of bringing others into that very same harmony.

All are in discord before they find Christ. But when Christ comes into one's life, discord is replaced by harmony. This is reconciliation. This is the kind of ministry we have been given. It was the ministry given to Jesus. Not only has He given us this ministry, but He has actually *committed* unto us the word of reconciliation.

Ministering In The Spirit's Power

The ministry comes through the power of the Spirit—not your spirit, but the Holy Spirit. God wants us to sacrifice ourselves that the life of His Son may be manifested. Paul says in Romans 12:1, "I beseech you therefore, brethren, by the mercies of God, that ye present your bodies a *living* sacrifice."

A sacrifice means something is put to death and laid on the altar. The Lord wants you to become a living sacrifice, voluntarily laying yourself on the altar, completely yielding to His Spirit, so that He can minister through you to others.

He calls this *your ministry*. But properly understood, it is not yours but His. "It is no longer I, but Him." Without the Holy Spirit, we cannot understand this, nor can we minister anything but the letter.

One Spirit With God

As we minister, we have fellowship with Him for we become one spirit together with Him. This intimate relationship brings us into a close association with Jesus. We walk with Him as His original disciples did, along the shores of the Sea of Galilee.

There must be low valley experiences as well as mountaintop experiences in this walk with God. But as we gain experience through the exercise of our senses, we mature. The valleys will be filled and the mountaintops will be leveled off. Our walk will become as serene as that of the Master Himself. In your maturity, others will not know when you are up or when you are down, for your walk will be steady and steadfast. The Spirit will be ministered powerfully and continuously.

We are the people of God. We know who we are and why we are here. We know that His will should be done on earth, even as it is done in heaven, and His name is to be exalted and glorified. Nothing can stand in the almighty presence of Jesus Christ, because He has already overcome the world and all the powers that are in this world. Through Him, God has made us more than conquerors as we minister His Spirit.

I want to encourage you to walk in the Spirit. You know that you walk in the Spirit if you walk in love, in peace, in joy, in meekness, in goodness, in faith, in longsuffering, and in gentleness. If you walk in these virtues, you walk in the Spirit. I want to encourage you to sacrifice your life as a ransom for many, being willing to die that others might live. I want to encourage you to do as Jesus did, for He came to minister unto, not to be ministered to, not to please Himself but to do the will of God.

CAST THY BREAD

"Cast thy bread upon the waters"—
    It shall return ten thousand fold!
Love, and Faith, and Prayer and Kindness
    Are more precious than Earth's gold!

Offer kindness to God's people
    Traveling through this weary vale;
Lift the weak, and broken-hearted;
    "Cast thy bread"—it shall not fail!

Give a helping hand to others
    Who are struggling in despair!
Point them to our loving Saviour
    Who will hear, and answer prayer!

What you give is never lost,
    If love is your motivation;
Compassion in the soul of man
    Came by the Lord of all creation!

"Once" we live! and "once" we die!
  Ah! How short Life's span of years!
Full of heartache and of sorrow;
  Filled with grief, and endless tears!

"Cast thy bread! Go, cast thy bread!"
  Only man's giving brings him peace!
God gave all, that we might find
  That giving brings to us increase!

"Cast thy bread upon the waters"—
  And unto the soul that prays,
You will find God will return it
  After many, many days!

"Cast thy bread" upon His waters—
  Let your soul unselfish be!
Christ was cast on cruel Calvary
  That His "breadlets" we might be!

Used by permission. From the book *Looking Unto Jesus* by Mabel Hogue Baker.